KATHLEEN HACKETT & MARY ANN YOUNG

THE
SALVAGE SISTERS'
GUIDE TO FINDING *style* IN THE STREET
AND *inspiration* IN THE ATTIC

ARTISAN
New York

"It is better to have looked and tossed than never to have looked at all." — The Salvage Sisters

We're not sure who spotted it first.

And we didn't care. The huge box of ball fringe with the five-dollar price tag literally brought us both to our knees. We crouched before it elbow-deep in skeins of fuchsia, tangerine, and grape-green trim that went unnoticed by the professional yard salers who had gathered at the end of the driveway well before the posted 8 A.M. start time. (We're not the types to storm the gates; rather, we take the relaxed approach, often picking up treasures on our way to somewhere else.) It was now 5 P.M. *Why hadn't anyone snagged this yet?* we wondered. *Probably reminds them of their grandmother's fussy tiebacks and pillow trims.* Kathleen untangled a bunch, wrapped it around her neck like a string of pearls, and continued to rifle through the stuff wearing her new jewelry. *Maybe there are great curtains underneath it all. Of course, we both knew, without saying a word to each other, that the last thing we would do with it was the expected:* sew it to the ends of bath towels or around the edges of café curtains or valances. No, these conservative cotton balls held more unique promise than that. Mary Ann wound yards and yards of the hot-pink fringe into globes of all sizes. *Won't these look cool in my dining-room cabinet?*

We stood up and dug around in our pockets for a five, then hauled the container to the car. Our excitement was outsize, and so was the box, so we pulled out the trim and stuffed it under the seats, among the baby gear, boogie boards, field hockey sticks, and life jackets—around us and between us—and returned the cardboard box to our friendly seller. And before we were strapped in and back on the road, our creative wheels began to turn. Within minutes, we had breathed life back into that ball fringe.

For as long as we sisters can remember, we have looked at the physical world through less-than-conventional lenses. Where someone else might see a tangled bunch of ball fringe, we see a clever cover for a quiet mantel (page 76) or outré ornamentation for a display of dishes (page 59). And then there are the stacks of newspaper. Most people let them pile up in a corner, tie them together, and recycle them. But to us, newsprint means a lot more, aesthetically speaking, than any pricey antique. There's almost nothing more gratifying than crumpling and folding and pinking the pages into chic decorations (page 107).

There's little we overlook on land or at sea, whether it's a castaway chair marooned on the curb or weathered pieces of driftwood washed up on the beach. We're compelled to stop, look, and imagine. And once we've given it our mental five-minute makeover—*just cut the ugly back right off that chair*—it's as if we've owned it all along, making the decision to haul it home or leave it behind a lot easier. *Having things isn't what necessarily makes our motors run; it's reimagining their lives—for the better—that energizes us.*

Where did we learn to appreciate the promise in even the most prosaic things? We come by our Salvage Sisters moniker honestly, maybe even genetically. And that's where our mother comes in. For someone who named all seven of her girls Mary (some now go by middle and nicknames) because she felt it was a simple, beautiful name, it's not surprising that she never took the expected approach to

The Salvage Sisters, circa 1966, pose for the annual family photo. That's Kathleen on the tiny tricycle and Mary Ann on the bike with the basket.

anything. She valued ingenuity and practicality equally, and though never a perfectionist, she infused even the most mundane moments with panache. It all appeared so effortless—it had to be, for a woman with nine children—yet no mother we knew could pull it together as she did.

Take, for instance, the family portraits she art directed each year. She artistically orchestrated all of us into position in a magnificent setting, whether it was on a snowbank, on a mountainside, or, as above, on ten bicycles (that's her on a Schwinn tandem with our father, who is holding Mary Margaret) in the driveway. Our mother's joie de vivre came through in everything she did—right down to a summer picnic of peanut butter and jelly sandwiches. She swirled that spread on the bread with the flair of a surrealist painter, spooning a dollop of jam in the middle the way Joan Miró might have if he put down his brush to take lunch. She dressed up the daily duties of life with flair, outfitting us all in red bathing suits in the summer, then swapping them out for red ski jackets in the winter. Always highlighting the expected with the unexpected, our mother relished putting bunches of dandelions we picked into one of our father's golf trophies and setting it on the dining-room table.

All nine of our birthdays were celebrated with the same cakes—they always leaned like the Tower of Pisa, and the frosting stuck to the knife—which delighted us every year, not least because she presented them as if to royalty. We never tired of those angel food cakes swathed in billowy seven-minute frosting and studded all over with spicy gumdrops, nor her pageantry of dimming the lights, carrying the candle-covered confection to the table slowly so that we could savor the flickering flames, or the rousing rendition of "Happy Birthday to You." Even her beloved black Labrador benefited from her wit: She used our grandmother's china for his dog bowls. And why not?

Now that we both have our own—much smaller—families, we realize our mother's efforts to instill in us the real meaning of beauty are nothing short of miraculous. Though we may not have been able to articulate it as young girls, the lessons we learned from her have now become crystal clear. Preeminent Parisian interior decorator and tastemaker Andrée Putman put in words what our mother embodied every day: "Unless you have a feeling for that secret knowledge that modest things can be more beautiful than anything expensive, you will never have style."

(Newspaper) hats off to you, Mother.

Why sit in a stroller when you can cruise around the neighborhood in a cast-off drawer? Finn delights in his ride while Kathleen and Stephen salvage city style.

The Swiss Family Robinson? No, it's just the Young family (from left, Mary Ann, Tom, Tom Tom, Jackie, and Mary Jane) gathering a few art supplies.

Like most mortals, we're occasionally stumped by a beautiful or quirky object that seems destined to be ours yet doesn't speak to us as clearly as, say, a beautiful old ball gown might: *Of course. Cut off the skirt and wrap it around a table* (page 81). It could be a set of old porch brackets with handsome curves, an inexpensive bolt of garden burlap with unbeatable texture, or even some great-looking plastic dishware from a discount retailer. Whenever we're stumped, we fall back on our mother's quirky brand of style for inspiration. An object's obvious purpose never stopped her from reinterpreting it to suit her personal taste—and needs. Rather than putting a single framed mirror over the fireplace, she pieced together various sizes and shapes of antique mirrors like a puzzle and fastened them to the wall, with no surround. And she always brought old garden furniture inside. Nothing was ever too corroded—she treated rust as a neutral color that went with everything. We both still covet the burnished camera case with the adjustable strap that she uses as a shoulder bag.

Admittedly, we are lucky to be sisters. It's rare to know someone who shares an almost identical vision, someone who has those *eureka!* moments when you do. For example, the instant you see the torn lamp shade, you both drop your jaw because you both know it will become a fantastic chandelier (page 96). Or, without hesitation, you hang pieces of garden burlap like rare lengths of silk in your living-room windows rather than draping those windows with store-bought—and too often uninspired—curtains (page 133).

Though we live more than four hundred miles apart from each other, it's as if we're right next door most days, together either on the coast of Maine or in New York City. We're passionate about both places, and we tend to live a little vicariously, stylewise, through each other. There's no rule against propping a tall driftwood-framed mirror on a brownstone's mantel or gracing a doorway in a Greek Revival home with a shredded-silk curtain, is there?

Occasionally, however, we have distinctly different ideas for the things we find. Butcher paper, for example, is the canvas on which Mary Ann's children paint playful scenes that she then hangs in her windows for curtains (page 131). Kathleen uses the same paper to make cones for holding individual servings of popcorn, spiced nuts, olives, and other simple hors d'oeuvres. We've included these alternate ideas and many more throughout the book.

Similarly, we don't always share the same methods for achieving our Salvage Sister madness, but we know one thing is certain: We're sure we drive type A personalities (and our husbands) to distraction. It's not that we don't appreciate perfection, but we're pragmatists at heart—too often the pursuit of it can obscure what truly brings us pleasure. Take tools, for example. In a recent phone call, Mary Ann gleefully declared that she was using her red wooden clog to pound a nail into the wall. The lobster cracker in her back pocket? It did a fine job of prying out old nails. Meanwhile, Kathleen was standing on a chest-of-drawers-turned-ladder to paint her living-room walls. Regardless, it's prudent to have on hand a glue gun, handsaw, electric drill (which also works as a screwdriver), hammer, needle and thread, and an assortment of hooks, screws, and nails. If necessary, however, we say it's okay to do things a bit off the cuff—or out of your back pocket, the toy box, or the silverware drawer.

By nature, we are sharers. And that's why we've filled the following pages with our favorite—and often funny—recasts of rusty salvage, forlorn furniture, discarded clothes, and common materials. Though some of our ideas may have a "they can't be serious" side, we are decidedly so, laughing all the way home. After all, without a good dose of wit and humor, we would just be living in rooms full of stuff. And it's not the stuff that gets us going. It's the shared experience of injecting beauty—and having a blast—into our lives every day. Now that's what makes us—and you, we hope—tick.

10 rules for Salvage Sisters

1 When in doubt, don't throw it out.

2 Rust is a variation of red;
red is *always* an acceptable color.

3 Never be the early bird at a yard sale.
The real *possibilities* are in the rubble.

4 Never sell among yourselves; trade only.
(It keeps that *sisterly love* alive.)

5 Broken? All the better. *Imperfect* is perfect.

6 Don't look at it for what it is,
but for what *it could be.*

7 It's about the *eureka!* moment, not the thing itself.

8 Make the recycling bin your first stop for art supplies.

9 Hunt, find, *and tell.*
No secret sources.

10 Never worry about how to get it home; *just get it.*

1. cool junk

ARCHITECTURAL SALVAGE IS REBORN

The stock French doors did a fine job of keeping the contents of Kathleen's rowdy closet from spilling out into the bedroom, but they lacked soul. New glass, bland handles, shiny hinges. *How can we give these two plain Janes a little panache?* It wasn't long before we spied our solution in the piles at an architectural salvage yard. Among the old columns, balusters, table legs, rotting doors, and rows of shutters that had been torn out of old buildings and put up for sale lay a perfectly patinated pediment that once graced the exterior of a Greek Revival home. *Is it really old or was it made to look old?* We hoisted the handsome piece out of the rubble and gave it a once-over. *Beautiful. Where should we put it?* Mary Ann had recently rehabbed her front porch, and it wasn't right for Kathleen's, but the gorgeously worn piece was too appealing to pass up. *Why not bring it inside?* Miraculously, it was just the right size for setting over Kathleen's closet doors.

When it comes to architectural salvage (and marine, for that matter), our bywords are borrowed from the great English bard: *"Things are seldom as they seem."* Nowhere in the Salvage Sister repertoire do we as gleefully assign new duties to castoffs as we do to the pieces in this chapter. Where in other sections we generally change or add something to a find in order to enhance its beauty—customize the legs on a chest of drawers, sew dressmaker details to a pair of occasional chairs—here our challenge is to give a castoff a whole new raison d'être.

There are the plant stands, for example, that make the most convenient and cunning aperitif or appetizer trays you'll ever come across (page 32) and the cast-iron lobster mold that has left the kitchen and turned up on the front door as an inventive knocker (page 23). In some cases, by simply bringing an object designed for the outdoors inside, it gets a second shot at life. Two Ionic columns that once held up a portico make a grand statement when you place one on either side of a bed (page 25). And if they are too far gone to stand on their own, you can cut them up crosswise in varying heights to make customized cake stands (page 28). An orphaned dory oar, too, can work in the great indoors. Fastened along the wall of a stairway, it becomes a useful handrail (page 41). Even a crumbling birdbath can find its way inside if you let it—and are strong enough to lug it! The textured basin, pitted from years of weathering, makes a beautiful centerpiece without holding a single thing or can function as a bowl for seasonal fruits and vegetables (page 38).

Our hope is that this chapter will inspire you to look at salvage not for what it is, but for what it can become. And when you're stumped, you might repeat our take on Shakespeare's famous phrase to call up your clever side.

knockout door knocker

Think cast-iron molds are just for making cornbread?

When we saw the lobster-shaped one, we knew we had to have it. After all, even a fair-weather Mainer (Kathleen) can't resist stuff rendered in the state's iconic crustacean. But it never crossed our minds to tack it up like a collection of Jell-O molds on the kitchen wall in Mary Ann's coastal Maine kitchen or Kathleen's nearby lakeside cottage. In fact, a Salvage Sister doesn't really go in for serious collecting; rather, she takes home anything that tickles her fancy. Unfortunately, this wasn't the kind of lobster we could share (Mary Ann gets the claws, Kathleen gets the tail), so we did the sisterly thing and put it where it belonged—on Mary Ann's front door. It faces the sea and is close enough to the road to charm passersby, and visitors get to see that it's not merely for display. The lobster mold, unearthed at a friend's live-in resale shop (we're not kidding; she sells the stuff right out from under herself), is mounted on the door with a hinge; just lift the tail to knock.

Mary Ann's classic Greek Revival front porch is a case study in salvagery. A piece of driftwood demurely does its job as a tablet for a house number, simply painted freehand with acrylic paint.

Those mercury glass balls? We found them in the garden ornament aisle of a local discount department store sitting atop resin cherub bases. We promptly discarded the bases and set the shiny globes in a pair of rusted urns, thrilled that they'll never need watering.

A hinge mounted beneath the eyes on the back of this lobster brings it back to life. A small piece of adhesive-backed felt protects the door from overeager knockers.

HOW TO MAKE A CAST-IRON MOLD INTO A DOOR KNOCKER

Look for a cast-iron mold that has a flat surface long enough to accommodate a hinge on one end and to hit the door on the other. Bring the mold to the hardware store to find the appropriate-size hinge, screws, bolts, and nuts.

materials

HINGE (½ TO 3 INCHES)

TREASURED CAST-IRON MOLD

PENCIL

ELECTRIC DRILL/DRIVER

CARBIDE-TIP DRILL BIT IN A SIZE APPROPRIATE TO THE HINGE HOLES

MEASURING TAPE

NUTS, BOLTS, SCREWS

ADHESIVE-BACKED PROTECTIVE FELT

1. Position the hinge at the top of the flat side of the mold. Using a pencil, make marks on the mold through the holes in the hinge to guide you when drilling through it.

2. Remove the hinge and, using an electric drill and a carbide-tip drill bit (designed specifically for use on metal), drill through the mold where the pencil marks are. Do not attach the hinge to the mold yet.

3. Position the mold where you want it on your door (ideally centered 16 to 18 inches from the top of the door). Using a dark pencil, mark the door through the holes in the mold. Using a drill and screws, fasten the hinge to the door at these pencil marks.

4. Place the mold on the hinge, lining up the holes in it with the holes in the hinge. Fasten the mold to the hinge with nuts and bolts.

5. We dabbed the screw heads with a bit of paint a color that closely approximated the rusted patina of the mold.

6. Gently use the door knocker, making note of where the bottom of the mold hits the door. Fasten a small, round piece of adhesive-backed protective felt in this spot to protect the door from dents and scratches—unless you like them!

floor-to-ceiling headboard

Two towering columns make a
mattress and box spring look positively palatial.

(page 27)

You can always find architectural salvage—just look for dealers in your yellow pages. But we aren't really the types to deliberately seek it out. Rather, we subscribe to the come-what-may approach; it's the serendipitous spotting of junk that makes it so attractive. Take, for example, the morning Mary Ann noticed five porch columns while driving her kids to school. They were sticking out of the back of a truck parked in front of a house that was for sale. Assuming the owners were getting rid of them, she tucked a note with her phone number under the windshield wiper on her way home. Minutes later, she got the call. For ten dollars each, the columns were hers, delivery to her door included. (Well, almost. That's us on pages 18–19, lugging one down the street.) What the owner saw as flaws in the aging porch columns, we viewed as virtues: They were beautifully beat up, ramrod straight, sitting on sturdy square bases, and covered in perfectly peeling paint. By positioning them at the head of a frameless bed—securing them by drilling pilot holes into each corner of the base and screwing them into the floor—the imposing pillars give the illusion of a grand headboard. And who knows, one day we might find two others at the foot of the bed to fashion a fabulous four-poster!

Mary Ann says Place two columns in the middle of a large room to delineate two cozier spaces. It's the perfect way to add a room—no contractor required.

Kathleen says Take a royal bath by setting two tall columns at either end of the bathtub. Add a shower curtain between the two to set the stage. A velvet one will make it feel like a theater when you open and close it.

Like a still-life painting, three angel food cakes rest on column remnants of varying heights. Pushing our salvage souls even further, we tucked a bouquet of shredded waxed paper into the center of each cake.

A curious sailor boy, appeared and took my hand, and led me only goodness knows where

Crumbling columns flank
either side of a basic bed to
give it serious status. Crisp
linens and a single painting
overhead keep lines clean,
making the chipped paint look
striking, not unsightly.

doggie decor

Make a best-in-show bedroom for the family pet.

Jackie, a Jack Russell terrier, is the baby in the Young family now that Mary Ann's daughter, Mary Jane, and son, Tom, are in their early teens. And believe us, Jackie gets red-carpet treatment at home (or Oriental carpet in this case). So when it came time to put together his bedroom—it's really just a transitional spot in the upstairs hallway—we put on the dog, fastening porch-railing balusters onto the floor with wood glue. To him, they're as princely as the pair his parents have (page 25). His nightstand? It's the base of the birdbath on page 38. For more information on how to make his fashionable sweater, hanging on the wall, see page 92.

cake stands that take the cake

Cut discarded porch columns down to size.

(page 26)

Here's proof positive that all architectural salvage can be saved. Our husbands have been around us long enough to know that before anything—and we mean *anything*—gets tossed, it gets the once-over from us. So when Mary Ann's husband, Tom, trimmed away a few good chunks from old columns he had specified for one of his porch designs, we saw petite pedestals where others would have seen pieces of debris. These inspired cake stands make milk glass and cut crystal look positively plain. Because the columns are hollow, place cakes on cut-to-fit cardboard rounds before setting them on their stands.

Jackie kicks back in a bedroom perfectly suited to his big-dog personality.

a spa closet

An old wine rack is swell for keeping supplies to pamper yourself.

It came out of the cellar, or *cave*, of a bistro in Paris, the man at the junk shop told us. And though we love the image of this wrought-iron cage housing bottle after bottle of the kind of wine one actually ages, our collection of "good" vintages combined would take up fewer than two slots. Still, this was too cool an object to ignore—not to mention relegate to the basement. So we paid the man and hoisted the thing on top of Mary Ann's jeep—no theatrics aside—and fled home on a few knots and a prayer. We never once fretted about where we would put it. After all, we never pay so much for something—nor is it ever so precious—that a misfit leaves us with any regrets. We talked about the rusty rack's possibilities—it went from being a garden shed to a bookcase to a shoe rack over the course of the ride—and then we agreed that a spa closet was what it needed to be.

Mary Ann says Duchamp probably didn't have one, but if he had, he might have used it to house his art supplies (and a little wine and his beloved chessboard, too) and called it a piece of art itself. Rolls of canvases and finished works slide perfectly onto the "shelves." Arrange a bouquet of brushes in a can on top and drape your painting apron over the open door.

Kathleen says Some shoes are worth displaying. Pull out your killer collection—from strappy high numbers to your favorite beat-up clogs—and show them off in the racks when you're not doing the two-step at the supper club. Of course, as when you're clothing yourself, the beauty is in the mix.

It used to live in a wine cellar, but we brought the old wrought-iron box alive in the bathroom by filling it with sparkling water and fresh towels. Mirrors set on top provide a gleaming surface for glasses and toiletries.

plant stands for everything but . . .

Plant these here, there, and everywhere.

It's not that we don't have green thumbs, it's just that if we had windows for every wrought- and cast-iron stand we own, we'd be living in a greenhouse. Why so many? Their uses are limitless. Those cleverly stepped shelves and platforms are perfect for portable hors d'oeuvres "buffets." The three-tiered design makes a great stand-alone tray for serving up a few snacks to your mate while making dinner; the more sprawling styles—with four or more arms—can be moved around the room to put appetizers at your guests' fingertips. Or you could put one in a bathroom, as we did, and elevate toilet tissue from utilitarian to outré. Try one in the guest bedroom, outfitted with a washcloth, soap, fresh flowers, and bottled water, or set one by a lounge chair at the pool and stock it with swim supplies—sun block, lip balm, spritz bottle, goggles, and bathing cap.

Mary Ann says Set a ringed version such as the one we used for toilet tissue just inside your back door for corralling the family's walking sticks, field and ice hockey sticks, baseball bats, tennis rackets, or soccer balls, depending on the season.

Kathleen says When you live in a walking city such as New York, having an umbrella is as much a necessity as it is an accessory; you can never own just one. Slide the umbrellas through the rings of a plant stand to put your collection at your fingertips, making selecting just the right one easier.

Why tuck toilet tissue behind closed doors when you can make an amusing arrangement of it in plain sight on a plant stand? The best part: There's no risk of unknowingly running out.

Step right up, sit right down: A rusted-out plant stand (opposite) makes a soigné serving tray, especially if it is set on a slick painted floor.

new old doors

Give mass a handsome touch of class.

Neoclass, that is. The old pediment crowning these French doors in Kathleen's room puts the Parthenon just within her reach. When your wallet forces you to settle for stock details like these doors (hey, they're not *that* bad!), give the gleaming expanse a handsome patina with a piece of architectural salvage. This wonderfully aged piece once graced the front door of a Federal-style home, but you can also use decorative headboards from tossed-out bed frames (twin beds are particularly easy to find, since they are not as desirable as they once were), fastening them over basic moldings and doors—even mirrors (page 61).

HOW TO HANG A PEDIMENT

materials

D-RINGS
OLD PEDIMENT
HEAVY-GAUGE WIRE
PENCIL
MEASURING TAPE
ELECTRIC DRILL/DRIVER
³⁄₁₆-INCH DRILL BIT
2-INCH LAG BOLT

1. Attach two picture-hook D-rings to the back side of the pediment at its apex. Use the screws included in the package.

2. Measure a length of heavy-gauge picture wire that is 10 inches longer than the width of the pediment. Thread it through the D-rings and pull 5 inches of wire through either side, then fold the ends back and twist them tightly around the main wire several times.

3. Place the pediment on the wall at the desired height. Mark the wall where the top of the pediment touches it. Set the pediment on a work surface and pull the picture wire toward the top until it is taut. Measure the distance between the top of the wire and the top of the pediment. Measure this same distance down from the mark on the wall and make a second mark.

4. With a ³⁄₁₆-inch drill bit, drill a pilot hole (a hole slightly smaller in diameter than the nail) at the second mark, where the top of the wire will hang. For heavy items like a pediment, this should be drilled into a stud in the wall (see the sidebar on page 37). Screw a 2-inch lag bolt (this looks like a giant screw with a hexagonal head) into the wall and stud and hang the pediment on it from the picture wire.

MIRROR, MIRROR, AND EVERYTHING ELSE HUNG ON A WALL . . .

We might use a clog to pound a nail, but we'd never skimp on the hardware necessary to safely hold up our stuff. Light- and medium-weight objects can be hung directly on drywall or plaster walls—they do not have to be anchored to a stud. Picture hooks nailed into the wall hold light items up to about twenty pounds. For medium-weight pieces, you have three choices: plastic anchors, hollow-wall anchors, and toggle bolts. Plastic anchors grip by expanding as you drive screws into them. It's important to drill the right-size hole for a snug fit. The hollow-wall styles spread open behind the wall surface for an installation that can't pull loose. Toggle bolts screw into wings that pop open inside the wall. You need to assemble them with the fixture before inserting. Hang heavy objects by nailing or screwing hangers into studs. For extra strength, nail a 1x4 between two studs, then nail or screw a picture hook to the 1x4.

Mary Ann says Give ordinary windows the royal treatment. There's nothing wrong with stock styles when you crown them with orphaned pediments. Put a different version over each window.

Kathleen says If you must put your Old Master in a new frame, the least you can do is age it a little. Mount a timeworn pediment and tell your friends it's been in the family for generations.

A perfectly pitched pediment hung over stock French doors gives Kathleen's closet a bit of cachet. Her wedding dress hangs on the wall; its shapely lines contrast beautifully with the classic architecture.

A mix of textures in a bathroom—sleek concrete meets chipping paint—gives a bathroom soul.

stylish sink supports

Porch brackets can hold up almost anything—even the bathroom sink.

Mary Ann found the perfect place for two peeling porch brackets without so much as getting out the tape measure. Mounted underneath a concrete console-style sink, they give the smooth surfaces surrounding them just enough roughness to warm up the room. And some styles are ideal for hiding ugly plumbing. The brackets don't bear the weight of the world, since they only *look* as though they're holding up the sink.

HOW TO FIND A WALL STUD

In many houses, the walls "hang" on a frame made up of vertical 2-inch by 6-inch pieces of wood known as studs. They are the sturdiest parts of the wall and, therefore, the safest spot to hang heavy pieces from. Most studs are spaced at regular 16- or 24-inch intervals. After you've found two, you can plot the others simply by measuring.

There are several ways to find that first stud. Begin the search near the wall's center. First, try knocking along the wall. A solid thud indicates a stud. Or look for nails in the baseboard. They're typically pounded into the studs. If both these methods fail, drill a tiny angled hole into the wall and probe with a stiff wire (a straightened coat hanger will do the job). Electronic stud finders can help, too, and are available at hardware stores. Once you've found the first stud, measure 16 inches (or 24 inches for some newer construction) in either direction to find the second.

Mary Ann says When you have more books than shelves, fasten two brackets to the wall over a doorway and set a 2x4 on top for a practical and pretty storage solution.

Kathleen says Brackets don't have to hold up anything more than a treasured memento or souvenir. Whether it's a plastic snow globe, a recent snapshot, or a note to a loved one, a bracket mounted in a place you pass by daily puts the things you cherish front and center.

HOW TO MOUNT BRACKETS UNDER A SINK

Avoid using heavy brackets (more than five pounds each) for this project unless you can fasten them to the studs behind the wall. The studs must be flush with the edges of the sink to mount the brackets properly. If you install the brackets before your sink is installed, use large flush-mount mirror hangers for the best fit; otherwise, use anchors and screws.

materials

PORCH BRACKETS
⅛-INCH DRILL BIT
ELECTRIC DRILL/DRIVER
PLASTIC ANCHORS
WITH CORRESPONDING SCREWS
HAMMER

1. Hold a bracket in position under the sink.

2. Using a ⅛-inch drill bit, drill through the thinnest part of the bracket until you just hit the wall, leaving a bit mark on the wall.

3. Insert a large plastic anchor as follows: Drill a hole of corresponding size into the wall at the bit mark and push in the anchor, tapping it with a hammer to make it flush with the wall. Hold the bracket in place and, using a screw that is long enough to go through the bracket and into the anchor, screw the bracket into the wall. Repeat with the remaining bracket.

not your average fruit bowl

An aging birdbath isn't for the birds.

There's almost nothing in the backyard that couldn't find a place inside our homes. This includes tree stumps, outdoor furniture, concrete urns—and decrepit birdbaths. This one was just barely standing in Mary Ann's backyard when the *eureka!* moment hit us. With a big chunk of the base missing, and the top and bottom of the column deeply cracked, the classic cement tub was too dangerous even for the boldest birds. So rather than encourage our feathered friends to swim at their own risk, we supplied them with a stable basin made from a hollowed rock, and rather than toss the forty-pound saucer, we lugged it inside and set it on the dining-room table, where it sits winter, spring, summer, and fall, filled with seasonal fruits, greens, a single floating flower, birthday gifts—or nothing at all. The crumbled pool has subtle patches of blue peeking through the craggy surfaces, making it a beautiful object all on its own. What'd we do with the remaining pieces? The base became Mary Ann's dog Jackie's bedside table (page 28). The Ionic column? Stay tuned.

The broad, bold stripes of a cotton tablecloth provide a graphic backdrop for the circular piece, filled with just a few lemons. There's no need to fill the basin to the brim.

A twelve-foot oar is the perfect length for a single flight of stairs.

oar indoors

Be inventive with overlooked spaces; put a paddle where a handrail would go.

It can help you row your boat ashore, but a dory oar's length will give you an even bigger boost stylewise along a stairway wall. Mounting an oar there is as simple as putting up any handrail. Using standard brackets from the local hardware store, simply fasten them to the wall 32 to 34 inches (that's the standard height) above the stair.

A bracket is screwed to a stud in the wall, then the oar is fastened to it with a bracket strap.

HOW TO MOUNT AN OAR ON THE WALL

materials

MEASURING TAPE

OAR

PENCIL

3 HANDRAIL BRACKETS
WITH ACCOMPANYING SCREWS

ELECTRIC DRILL/DRIVER

1. Measure the length of the oar from just above the loom (where the paddle shape begins) to the end of the handle. Mark this measurement in the desired place on the wall. Find three studs along this measurement; one bracket will be attached to each of them. Measure the distance between the studs, then mark this distance on the oar handle to mark the placement of the brackets.

2. Ideally, the 3 brackets should be spaced an equal distance from either end of the oar handle, but it's more important that the brackets be fastened securely to the wall.

3. With the electric driver, screw the brackets to the wall at the designated points. Then lay the oar on the brackets and fasten with the bracket straps and screws.

41

rope railing

Retired dock line is for landlubbers, too.

You don't have to be a nautical know-it-all to check out the marine salvage stores. They're especially exciting places for those of us who live in small spaces, since most things featured in the stores are designed to be superefficient, not to mention stand up to a lot of wear and tear. This heavy-duty dock line was once tied to a tugboat to aid in towing other boats, but it makes a perfect railing inside Kathleen's lakeside cottage (it could be used along an outdoor stairway, too). By threading it through pipe brackets (available at the hardware store) and positioning them so that you can screw them into the studs in the wall (see page 37), you can shape a stair rail in a space where previously there might have been a mass-produced, style-starved straight version.

"You shall never want rope enough."

— Françoise Rabelais

Old rope lends a lyrical rhythm
to the wall along the staircase
in Kathleen's cottage.

2. big stuff

FURNITURE GETS A FACE-LIFT

The neighbors looked on, aghast yet intrigued. Why would anyone ever saw the back off a perfectly good chair? Passersby peered up the driveway, mesmerized. Why are those girls laughing so hard? We were just doing what it took to turn a pair of homely chairs into good-looking ones. And these particular numbers (page 54), with their gangly backs and outsize scrolled headrests, needed some serious surgery.

Two minutes was all the time we needed to determine that the twin chairs were worth wrestling into the car. They had good legs, the seat and arms were nicely proportioned, and there were two of them. *But those backs!* Mary Ann sat in one chair, Kathleen in the other, and imagined how they might look if cut down to size. We agreed that these ugly ducklings could, indeed, become swans.

Once home, we drew a straight line all around the top of each chair with tailor's chalk, then cut into the fabric and foam with a razor until we hit the frame. With electric saw in hand, we trimmed the chairs of their outdated shape, and their new life began.

Most of the time, providence provides us with the most intriguing pieces. One day several years ago, for example, while we were cruising around in Mary Ann's station wagon—the ultimate hauling vehicle—we spotted a man tossing furniture out onto his front lawn. *Is he moving out?* When the cute little love seat with the not-so-lovely upholstery landed on the grass, we had to pull over. Indeed, the guy was preparing for a yard sale the following day, but would we like to buy anything now? We gave him a twenty, tossed the granny green sofa onto the roof of the car, and strapped it down with clothesline. After covering it forty different ways in our minds, we ended up tossing an exquisite piece of silk from a Paris flea market over it and leaving it at that.

And that's our highly scientific method for making that nagging decision: *Should I lug it or leave it?* When it comes to the big stuff—couches, chests of drawers, shelving units, and cabinets—it's more tempting to haul the hulking things home when you have more or less specific plans for them. Though we dislike having to make on-the-spot aesthetic decisions, there's nothing like the specter of some heavy lifting to get our creative juices going.

Why did we decide that a settee with only three legs (page 49) was worth flexing our collective muscles for? Its scale is sweet, and we never worry about missing feet. A stack of books stands in quite nicely. And what were we thinking when we weighed down Kathleen's car with a pair of 150-pound cabinets? A few coats of bold paint would enhance the "bamboo" lines while handsomely covering up the ugly faux-wood-grain surfaces (page 55).

We do have a few regrets, of course. There was the Marcel Breuer–like chrome chair with the strappy leather armrests that was pitched out in front of a Brooklyn brownstone. We had a mile-long list of errands to do that day and no time to drag it back home. *Maybe that guy sitting on his stoop will tuck it under the stairs for us.* "*Mais, oui,*" the man responded in his native French as he gave the chair a once-over. "*C'est jolie.*" Unfortunately, someone else thought so, too, and by the time we turned around, the chair had vanished. *Strike while the iron's hot.*

And let's not forget the pieces of furniture we already have. Who doesn't own a few chairs that need a little TLC? What would a Salvage Sister do? Toss cheap-but-chic cheetah-print fleece throws over them and have a seat (page 50).

As Salvage Sisters, we have especially soft spots for the abandoned, orphaned, and cast-off. This can sometimes lead to carrying excess baggage, but in the case of single drawers separated from their chests, it can also lead to a sculptural take on a bookcase that you will never find in any catalog (page 66). And that's the beauty of bringing home the big things—with a little effort, you can create a lot of individual style.

Mary Jane is sitting pretty under her self-portrait on her new couch with the clever leg.

improvised couch leg

When a couch is missing a leg,
look on the bright side: It comes with three!

We spotted this couch on a city sidewalk one blistering summer afternoon. It just lay there, one front leg shooting skyward because one back leg was no longer there. Pity the fool who tossed this lovely little settee in the trash—it's perfectly

scaled for small-space living, leg or no leg. It's also just the right size for two smallish women to haul home. Mary Ann slipcovered it (a modest attempt, she would admit) and set it up in a corner, still peg-legged, then slid a color-coordinated selection of favorite books underneath to shore it up.

A half dozen books stack up to a sturdy leg on a library couch.

small idea

writerly window prop

It's the same old story: A century-old house comes with old windows that don't always stay up. But it's nothing to get frustrated about. Not when an enduring classic can carry the weight and let in a little breeze, too.

chair of blooms

Plant a flower bed on a bare chair for real flair.

We could have left the perforated seat on this faux bamboo chair plain, but it wouldn't delight us nearly as much as a garden of blowsy flowers. We clipped the stems off of a bouquet of old silk roses, then poked them through the holes of the wicker seat. That's it. When the summer turns to fall, we can pick them with abandon and tuck some autumn leaves in their place. (If you invite visitors to sit among the flowers, glue the blooms to the seat with a hot-glue gun.)

two-second slipcover

When upholstered chairs tear, give them an instant makeover.

(page 52)

Hey, it's not that we don't know these chairs need a good reupholstering job, but they're used day in and day out, and dropping them off at an upholstery shop (never mind loading them into the car) and living without them would make life complicated. So rather than doing the right thing and repairing them, we rid ourselves of the eyesores by draping an animal-print throw made from a five-foot-square piece of wash-and-wear polar fleece blanket over each one. In no time at all, we gave two tattered chairs a lot of flair.

Mary Ann says Take that shaggy rug up off the floor and throw it over a forlorn chair to give it a certain "je ne sais quoi."

Kathleen says You know that pretty skirt that you never wear? Pull it out of your closet and drape it over the frayed arm of a chair.

Nothing beats a bed of roses—
except a chocolate painted
chair covered in a field of hot
pink peonies.

No dry cleaning necessary for
these slipcovers (opposite).
Two six-dollar fleece blankets
hide the sartorial sins of these
family-room chairs.

Private eye? No, that's just
Jackie comparing the quality of
his faux fur hat to the buttons
on the back of his chair.

extreme chair makeover

Cut a pair of ugly chairs down to size to make them chic—and more comfortable, too.

We're not afraid to take outlandish measures to turn run-of-the-mill furniture into unique designs. And we're not too timid to turn on the switch of a reciprocating saw (the construction equivalent of a food processor—the blade moves back and forth for you). What, you may wonder, did we see in these off-scale chairs in the first place? The fabric's traditional pattern and color didn't dissuade us at all. And a peek underneath the skirt revealed some not-so-bad legs—at least they were in scale. It was the Dr. Seuss–like style and height of the backrest that forced us to mentally draw the line. By cutting off the scrolled headrest, we turned a bland piece of showroom furniture into a designer's delight. Once we sawed them into shape, we covered the chairs in color-drenched raw silk, then gave each one faux-fur buttons for a bit of humor and arm patches for practicality.

HOW TO CHANGE THE LINES— AND LIFE—OF A CHAIR

We use the conversation chairs as an example here, but the process can apply to most upholstered or slipcovered pieces. The secret is in creating a new silhouette. We're not big on upholstering (The precision! The patience! The time!), so we recommend using a professional for a seamless look.

materials
MEASURING TAPE
TAILOR'S CHALK
BOX CUTTER OR DRYWALL KNIFE
RECIPROCATING SAW
STAPLE GUN

optional
SCISSORS
3 YARDS FAUX FUR
OVERSIZE BUTTONS
FABRIC GLUE
PINS
NEEDLE AND THREAD

1. Using a measuring tape and tailor's chalk, make a straight line around the front and back of the backrest at the desired height. Make a second line about 1½ inches above it.

2. With a box cutter or drywall knife, cut into the fabric along the top chalk line, exposing the wood frame.

3. Measure and mark the frame where you plan to chop off the backrest. Then, using a reciprocating saw, cut it off across the back.

4. Lay the excess foam and fabric over the top of the cut-off frame and toward the back of the chair. Fasten it with a staple gun to prepare it for upholstering or slipcovering. (Again, we recommend having a professional make your slipcovers or reupholster.)

5. After you've had the chair upholstered, add your own dressmaker details: Cut oval patches from faux fur and affix them to the arms using fabric glue. Don't stop there. Tack oversize buttons down the back, too: Cut six 8-inch by 2½-inch strips of faux fur. Roll each one fur side out, as you would a jellyroll, and use fabric glue to hold it together. Center 3 fur buttons vertically down the back of each chair and pin them in place. Hand sew them onto the fabric.

handsome wardrobes

Faux-bamboo breakfronts get a face-lift with bold coats of paint.

(pages 56–57)

It's hard to see anything among the mountains of junk at Sydney's, a block-long warehouse in Brooklyn, New York. The single-story space is filled from floor to ceiling with furniture, records, dolls, bicycles, coffee mugs, and every other household item under the sun. But beyond the broken lamps and office chairs, we spied a pair of faux-bamboo cabinets with surprisingly refined lines—rare for this style, since most sport the cartoonish proportions that scream furniture store. Unfazed by the ugly stained wood and the decorative borders on the doors, we freed them from their bric-a-brac trap and, with a brilliant combination of paint colors, a bit of wrapping paper, and a little word play, Kathleen got herself a set of spiffy new wardrobes. You can transform practically any piece of furniture (from Sydney's or anywhere else) this way. Using an artist's brush and a bit of primer, we handwrote a word (we're never afraid to show our silly side) on the crown of each cabinet.

Junk

Two cabinets, one for holding
"junk," the other for harboring
"stuff," are coated in high-
gloss Bittersweet Chocolate
by Benjamin Moore. Curtains
of brilliant fuchsia wrapping
paper with an Asian motif
hide it all.

Stuff

dazzling dish cabinet

Now here's a china cupboard we can live with.

Salvage Sisters always keep an open mind, especially when it comes to how to use their furniture. So when Kathleen realized that her side-by-side wardrobes (page 55) were taking up too much space, she hauled one into the living room and finally had a place for her dishes—and a few mementos. We kept the deep chocolate shade on the outside, removed the paper curtains, and gave the interior a wash of Inner Glow, a stunning chartreuse high-gloss paint by Benjamin Moore.

A fresh coat of bright paint on the inside of a cabinet provides a slick backdrop for a not-so-serious collection of white pieces Kathleen and Stephen received as wedding gifts. Watching over it all? A gauze-veiled bride in a white felt dress and her dapper groom.

HOW TO PAINT FURNITURE LIKE A PRO

For these cabinets, we applied high-gloss paint for its lustrous sheen (it covers a multitude of sins, too), using 4-inch premium sponge rollers to achieve a supersmooth surface.

materials

ELECTRIC DRILL/DRIVER

FINE-GRIT (#220) SANDPAPER

PAINTBRUSH (1½ INCHES WIDE)

PRIMER

4-INCH SPONGE ROLLERS

PAINT

ARTIST'S BRUSH

1. Using an electric drill/driver, remove all the hardware. Set aside.

2. Lightly sand all the surfaces with fine-grit sandpaper, roughing them up slightly so the paint adheres to the surfaces.

3. Paint the cabinets inside and out with primer. Leave the doors open to dry.

4. Roll on the paint and let it dry—the time will vary depending on humidity and temperature—from 4 hours or overnight. If you wish, use an artist's brush and a bit of primer to handwrite a word or name or whatever on the crown of each cabinet.

most-improved mirrors

Put a little paint on a dime-a-dozen-style mirror or rescue a shard.

This mirror was once your basic ersatz Chippendale model (page 89), which on a whim Mary Ann trimmed in newspaper (page 111). When it came time to put the mirror in its final resting place in her seaside home, she removed the newspaper and gave it a wash with aqua paint to relieve it of a bit of its stodginess. To apply the wash, she painted around the frame with a turpentine-soaked brush dabbed in a bit of Benjamin Moore Jamaican Aqua enamel.

Sometimes the parts of a mirror are better than the whole. You could toss the pieces in the trash, or you could see that some are serendipitously separated into shapes you recognize—and love. To someone who lives by the sea, the triangular chunks beautifully reflect the local harbor landscape.

A shining sail pulled from a pile of cracked mirror pieces (above) floats in front of an aqua blue sky inside a tiny cabinet.

A wash of color gives a mundane mirror (right) a face-lift.

bland mirror, beautiful flourish

The fairest of them all has a good-looking crown.

This plain old ordinary rectangular mirror would look, well, ordinary if it weren't for the carved scallop-shell crown on top. Once the decorative trim on a headboard for a twin bed, it was on its way to the junk pile until we intervened. Though neither of us needed a twin bed, there was something about the headboard that compelled us to hand over the ten-dollar asking price. The headboard turned out to be the same width as a boring mirror hanging in Kathleen's cabin, so, with a swipe of the circular saw and a few brackets and screws, we had ourselves a custom looking glass.

An unwanted headboard (above) plus a plain mirror equal a one-of-a-kind creation.

The hinges are mounted vertically on the back between the crown and the mirror (right).

HOW TO MOUNT HEADBOARD TRIM ON A MIRROR

materials

PENCIL
YARDSTICK
TWIN HEADBOARD
CIRCULAR SAW OR HANDSAW
PLAIN SQUARE OR RECTANGULAR MIRROR
TWO 2-INCH HINGES OR MENDING PLATES
FOUR TO EIGHT ½-INCH WOOD SCREWS
ELECTRIC DRILL/DRIVER
PAINT (OPTIONAL)

1. Use a pencil and a yardstick or other straightedge to mark where to cut the crown off the headboard.

2. Trim the crown from the headboard. We used a circular saw, which guarantees a smooth cut, but a handsaw will do the job, too, as long as you make a straight, even cut.

3. Lay the mirror facedown and position the crown facedown and centered over the top of the mirror.

4. Using hinges or mending plates (they're the hardware equivalent of butterfly bandages and are easy to find at your local hardware store) and ½-inch wood screws, fasten the two pieces together by placing the hinges or plates an equal distance apart along the seam formed where the two pieces of wood meet, then drilling the screws through them and into each piece.

5. We painted the mirror and crown to give it a cohesive look, but you can decide how to finish your own. Wire and hang the mirror as directed for the pediment on page 34.

a boy's bureau

Customize a mass-produced chest of drawers with a box and some rocks.

We love the basic furniture at IKEA—not because we're minimalists (hardly), but because it provides a blank canvas for us to put our personal stamp on. Take, for example, the Lo style children's chest of drawers. We made it much more interesting for Tom Tom's room by taking our cues from his passion for the sea. First, we painted the whole thing driftwood gray. Then we stacked flat rocks and secured one on top of the other with epoxy glue to replace the two front legs. We painted our grandmother's old silver flatware box aqua blue and mounted it on top of the chest with wood glue (you can just set it on top if you prefer). It's perfect for holding a little boy's rotating collection of sea treasures.

A fascination with all things aquatic inspired the embellishments on Tom Tom's basic dresser. Stacks of smooth, flat rocks make great feet (opposite), while our grandmother's pine silver box (right) comes with slots all ready for sorting collections (far right).

to-die-for dish display

Don't ditch fuddy-duddy dishes. Display them with a designer's touch.

Wouldn't it be great if you could trade in your old wedding china for dishes that better reflect your current style? Not really. Why pitch all those pieces you once loved when you can make them part of a display that reveals your confidence, wisdom, and humor? Mary Ann still has a sentimental attachment to—and appreciation for the design of—her decades-old wedding china, but the gold-banded Louvecienne Limoges with its swags of greenery, pink roses, and delicate French blue flowers wouldn't be her first choice today. Still, she wasn't about to put it all in a box and stash it away in the attic. Rather, we put it together with a bunch of hot pink plasticware from a discount retailer, and with that, the dated dishes looked positively dashing.

This cabinet (opposite) appears to be full of traditional china, but a closer look reveals that plastic compotes, plates, cups, and a punch bowl offset the finer pieces. We built the cake stands ourselves from an overturned cup and bowl, each topped with a plate.

A plastic compote, tumbler, and pilsner lend a bit of humor to the more serious side of a china cabinet. To give the cabinet a less "granny" appearance, we slid boldly colored plastic plates behind the delicate pieces.

brilliant bookcases

Cast-off drawers begin life again as built-in bookcases.

Loose drawers are the urban equivalent of driftwood—they seem to show up on New York City curbs no matter what the address, some pleasingly worn, others too new looking, and still others too far gone. Kathleen picks them up with the same hunter-gatherer spirit that Mary Ann applies to driftwood (page 124). Like seaside treasures, some drawers are better for the taking than others. What could we possibly do with a bunch of mismatched ones, you wonder? We put them together to make a custom bookcase that is both beautiful and functional. If you're as lucky as we are, you'll find drawers in sizes to suit every odd-shaped book you own.

(continued)

Finn plays a real-life jack-in-the-box in a loose drawer his dad found on the street.

Assorted drawers add up to an artful bookcase (opposite).

HOW TO MAKE A BOOKCASE FROM ORPHANED DRAWERS

You can build an entire bookcase all at once if you have enough drawers, or you can let it grow more dynamically by attaching them to the wall as you find them. This approach may not yield a snug fit, but that would never bother us. In some cases, you may have to trim the face of the drawer to be flush with the bottom and sides.

materials

MISMATCHED DRAWERS

ELECTRIC DRILL/DRIVER

3/8-INCH DRILL BIT

MEASURING TAPE

3/8-INCH BOLTS
(1¼ TO 1½ INCHES LONG)

CORRESPONDING WASHERS AND NUTS

ONE 1X4 CUT APPROXIMATELY
4 INCHES SHORTER THAN
THE LENGTH OF THE BOOKCASE

1¼-INCH WOOD SCREWS

1. Lay the drawers out on the open face side up and arrange them as if you were doing a puzzle, keeping in mind the wall space that you intend to mount them on.

2. Using a drill with a 3/8-inch bit, drill holes at 12-inch intervals through 2 drawers wherever they are going to be attached to each other, both horizontally and vertically.

3. Slide the smaller washer onto the 3/8-inch bolt (1¼ or 1½ inches long, depending on the thickness of the wood), then thread the bolt through each hole. Slide the large washer onto the nut, then screw the bolt tightly to fasten.

BOLT

WASHERS

NUT

4. To mount the finished bookcase on the wall, screw a 1x4 piece of pine (or any other wood you desire) into the wall studs (page 37). This is necessary to safely secure the bookcase to the wall. (Note: If your bookcase is multitiered and will be holding lots of heavy stuff, consider fastening one 1x4 for each tier.)

5. Measure the distance between where the top of the bookcase will go and the middle of the 1x4. Mark off this same measure on the inside of the bookcase, every 12 inches. This is where you will screw it to the 1x4.

6. Have two people hold the bookcase in place and, using the electric drill and 1¼-inch wood screws, fasten the unit to the 1x4.

Mary Ann says Don't keep those mementos tucked away. Pull them out and arrange them in a loose drawer, have a piece of glass cut to fit on top, and fasten some feet on the bottom for a curio coffee table.

Kathleen says A tiny drawer mounted on the wall is perfect for holding a roll of toilet paper, especially when you live in a storage-starved apartment.

"There are many things that we would THROW AWAY *if we were not afraid* OTHERS MIGHT PICK THEM UP."

— Oscar Wilde

3. good goods

NEW LIFE FOR CLOTHES, CURTAINS, AND CLOTH

We were feeling so altruistic. There's nothing like donating a healthy pile of old clothes—a buffalo plaid hunting vest *(where did that come from?)*, a pair of hockey skates, an old winter coat—to Goodwill. We stood in the parking lot with corduroy gauchos, 1970s ski jackets, and bulky sweaters piled in our arms, about to head for the big metal box and looking forward to that lightweight feeling that cleaning out your closets brings. But before we slid a single garment into the receptacle, Mary Ann dropped her stack of clothes and shot Kathleen that familiar look. *Do you see what I see?* Candy-pink organdy and tulle layers were caught in the donation bin's door—and they were only a tiny fraction of the story. Kathleen pulled down the door as Mary Ann, standing on her tiptoes, gently wriggled the fabric free. *I wonder how much there is?* It only got better. With a final tug, the pink confection revealed itself in all of its magnificent ball-gown glory. Silk flowers floated between layers of organdy and tulle. *Who wore such a chic number? And where did she wear it?* We held the full-skirted frock up to each other. *It's a work of art.* It didn't matter that neither of us had had a need for such a gown since the junior prom. Mary Ann hugged the dress in her arms. We couldn't possibly cut it up. It was just begging for a second life. *Why not just hang it on the wall?*

And who says that a beautifully constructed dress can't grace a barren wall like a fine tapestry might? Or, fit around a table to make an elegant skirt (page 81)? Clothing, scraps of fabric, and notions have long been among our favorite treasures to squirrel away (thus the trip to the Goodwill bin, but it helps if you have a sister who can hoist you up) and are, in fact, some of the easiest items for novice salvagers to handle. They generally don't require special transportation—you can carry them home on foot if you have to—they don't take up a lot of space, and, if inspiration fails you, they can always be used for one-of-a-kind pillows or shredded and used for wrapping around gifts. There's really only one rule of thumb when it comes to snapping up or saving fabric and clothing: Only hang on to pieces that have patterns, textures, or colors that you really love.

Consider the orange cashmere sweater Kathleen couldn't part with. She loved the feeling of the soft wool on her skin, but the fit did nothing for her. Into the back of the closet it went—until she realized that Mary Ann's Jack Russell terrier is about the size of its sleeves. He now proudly wears a sweater fashioned from one of its arms. Similarly, Mary Ann filed away a pair of plaid pegged pants (nice pattern, not-so-nice cut) that one day became a dashing bow tie for her son. Only she knew enough to save those pants; she loved the red plaid. Not only fine fabrics are worth keeping; one of our favorite—and most poignant—projects in this chapter is crafted from that most common cloth, denim. By cutting up some forlorn pieces of everyday clothing, including jeans, corduroys, and cotton broadcloth shirts, we stitched together a quilt that will be a lasting reminder of the family members whose pockets, plackets, and patches are pieced into it. By reshaping those scraps of fabric, we brought a pile of clothes back to life in a beautiful, useful way, and that's the true essence of a Salvage Sister.

humorous holiday decor

You can have a ball with ball fringe.

What happens when you give a couple of girls a box of ball fringe and a little too much caffeine? They come down with a bad case of irrational exuberance.

Perhaps you've seen this fringelike trim on colonial-style café curtains or looped around heavy drapes. Rather than using it for pedestrian adornment, why not showcase it as sculpture? If you have a collection of eclectic dishes and beloved tchotchkes, you're already one style step ahead. But how can you pull that crazy array of plates and cups, platters and pooches together to turn it into a style statement nonpareil? The clever placement of varying sizes and colors of ball-fringe globes does the trick as long as you're willing to go a bit over the top. You don't have to wait until some shows up at a yard sale, as we did. Most fabric stores sell ball fringe, but for a wider range of hues, try a specialty trim store.

A Salvage Sister doesn't toss out family china or gifts that mark sentimental milestones, no matter what the current trend or her changing style. Though it includes several pieces some would call stodgy, Mary Ann's dish display is anything but. Leaving no bare spot unembellished, we gave the regal Staffordshire dog a Louis-Philippe "do," while the tinier pooch got a supertall top hat. Under the cheese dome? A bunch of grapes fashioned from spring green ball fringe. We tied it into knots to make a stopper for the decanter and tied a length into a bow to adorn the tall neck of an aperitif bottle. Rather than piling predictable real fruit on the compote, we wound the stuff into a single piece of pom-pom fruit the size of a bowling ball. The tiny teacups hold the leftovers.

Pom-poms with pizazz perk up an antique cabinet filled with heirloom pieces.

HOW TO WORK WITH BALL FRINGE

materials

OLD FIGURINES
LENGTHS OF BALL FRINGE
LENGTHS OF CORDING
HOT-GLUE GUN

To give a dog (or any other statue or figurine) long hair, cut lengths of ball fringe and use a hot-glue gun to attach them to the pup's head. To make a hat, cut pom-poms off the band of fringe and use a hot-glue gun to attach them one by one in a pyramid shape.

Make globes in various sizes in the same way you would make a ball of yarn. Wrap ball fringe loosely around your hand a few times, then slide it off and continue wrapping to create a globular shape.

A limited palette of hot pink, forest green, and a mix of spring and apple green keeps Kathleen's mantel looking sophisticated without being too serious. The contemplative plaster nun sets a serene mood, despite the explosive colors in her midst.

deck the walls, mantel, and sconces

Swathe a quiet mantel in colorful ball fringe.

(pages 76–77)

Pretty pewter walls and an elegant marble fireplace make Kathleen's living room the perfect backdrop for a playful take on traditional mantel decoration. So with glue gun in hand, we made a magnificent wreath from fuchsia ball fringe and hung it dead center, then stuffed tiny cast-iron urns with too-tall topiaries growing out of them. As a final flourish, we gave the French wrought-iron sconces a softer side, shades and all, and added our own drippy fringe from each candlestick.

Jackie plays the fashion hound in his pom-pom leash.

HOW TO MAKE BALL-FRINGE TOPIARIES

materials

LEGAL-SIZE MANILA FOLDERS OR PLASTIC-FOAM CRAFT FORMS

2 YARDS BALL FRINGE

HOT-GLUE GUN

1. Roll a legal-size manila folder lengthwise into a cone shape, manipulating it to fit into whatever vessel you are using. Glue it along the seam to hold it together. Alternatively, you can trim plastic-foam forms to the shape you desire (however, you may not be able to get the height pictured on pages 76–77).

2. Cut individual pom-poms off the fringe and glue them, one at a time, onto the cone until the entire surface is covered. We used two shades of green to give the topiaries dimension.

We used a 36-inch circular stretched canvas from an art supply store as a base for this wreath. It is available in smaller sizes, too, so use whatever size you prefer.

materials

36-INCH CIRCULAR STRETCHED CANVAS

MEDIUM-GRIT (#100) SANDPAPER

30 YARDS BALL FRINGE

HOT-GLUE GUN

CORDING TO MATCH BALL FRINGE

3-INCH NAIL, HEAVY-GUAGE PICTURE HANGER
OR DRYWALL ANCHOR

1. Sand the surface of the canvas with medium-grit sandpaper. This is necessary to "lift" the fibers on the canvas, giving the glue something to grip on to.

2. Working with one length of ball fringe at a time, shape the fringe into tightly packed flower petals and glue them around the canvas, one layer at a time. Continue shaping petals and attaching them to the canvas until none of its surface shows through. Overlapping is necessary to cover the form entirely and to add dimension.

3. Secure any droopy loops with more hot glue.

4. To fill the center, wind lengths of the cording into loops and glue them in the center of the wreath until it is completely covered.

5. To hang the wreath Salvage Sister style, pound a 3-inch nail into a stud in the wall (see page 37) and let the inner rim of the canvas rest right on it. If the stud is not in the right spot, use a heavy-gauge picture hanger or a drywall anchor.

HOW TO MAKE BALL-FRINGE SCONCES

You can cover the shades on your sconces permanently or just for the holiday season. If you're gutsy (and your shades aren't worth a fortune), just clip the fringe into individual balls and hot-glue them in bands, beginning at the bottom and gluing your way to the top. For a temporary splash of color, use a paper clip to fasten a length of ball fringe at the back of the shade's bottom, then wind it around until the whole shade is covered. Fasten the end of the length of ball fringe to the back of the top with a second paper clip.

To cover the wrought-iron braces, we simply hot-glued ball fringe directly on them and glued individual lengths underneath each stem as final flourishes.

Mary Ann says Don't resort to wrapping unimaginative ribbon around gifts. Tie them with tons of ball fringe to give presents with presence.

Kathleen says So what if the baubles in Tiffany's windows are out of reach. A bunch of ball fringe will turn heads when you wind it around and around and around your neck.

Every time she sees the tulle overlay on her dressing table, Kathleen wants to twirl around the room. Her baby boy, Finn, is happy that his mom has a place to relax and play with him.

haute couture table skirt

Drape an old ball gown on a dressing table.

Okay, so you don't have an official boudoir and neither do we, but once we pulled this beautiful ball gown out of the drop-off bin at Goodwill (we work in reverse; we make withdrawals before making deposits) there was little we could do to contain ourselves. The idea that this organdy and tulle masterpiece, complete with silk orchids sewn between the layers, was orphaned just killed us. Forgetting that we retired our tiaras in 1978 after a final recital at Miss Lorraine's School of Dance, we took the divine dress home with us. Mary Ann put it on right away and pretended she was a princess. But after a quick sisterly consult, Kathleen was cutting the dress off her sister with visions of a stunning table skirt in her head.

We prefer a 36-inch round table for this transformation. Don't worry if the skirt doesn't fully cover the table; the back and top can be covered in a fabric of the same color—just push the table up against a wall. If you find (or have) a petite dress, wrap it around the rim of a small sink or boudoir stool. If you can't bear to cut it up, hang it on the wall as if it were your everyday overcoat and call it art. The directions below are for a skirt that goes around the entire circumference of a table.

materials

36-INCH ROUND TABLECLOTH

36-INCH ROUND TABLE

SCISSORS

GATHERED BALL GOWN
WITH VERY FULL SKIRT

IRON

STRAIGHT PINS

NEEDLE AND THREAD

1. Drape the tablecloth over the table.

2. Cut the skirt of the gown away from the bodice about 1 inch above the seam. Make a 1-inch fold along the seam to the wrong side of the fabric and press. Using straight pins, attach the wrong side of the skirt to the right side of the cloth.

3. Using a whip stitch, hand sew the skirt to the tablecloth along the top of the table's edge. Position the table with the skirt facing front. Fiddle with the skirt, pulling it away from the table to make it look as full as possible. Run your hands around the hem.

the quintessential family quilt
It's in the jeans—or corduroys or khakis.

In early 2002, we were lucky enough to see one of the most poignant and awe-inspiring museum shows in our collective lifetimes: The Quilts of Gee's Bend. The remarkable quilts we contemplated that day at New York's Whitney Museum of American Art will forever remain an inspiration to us. Handmade by six generations of women living in Gee's Bend, Alabama, a tiny rural community nestled in a curve in the Alabama River, the haphazardly designed pieces gave the words *Salvage Sisters* brand-new meaning. These women crafted distinctive, bold, and sophisticated quilts from whatever scraps of fabric they could find, including old canvas pants, jeans, corduroy, and mattress ticking. Their style moved art critics worldwide to compare their work to that of Henri Matisse and Paul Klee. *The New York Times* called the quilts "some of the most miraculous works of modern art America has produced." So here, in our homage to the women of Gee's Bend, is Mary Ann's family quilt, crafted from her husband's jeans and old corduroys and backed with one of his old, supersoft white button-down shirts.

Mary Ann says By the way, a quilt isn't just for covering a bed. Take it into the dining room and drape it over the table.

Kathleen says Put up your feet on an ottoman covered in well-worn and familiar fabric—pieces of your family's old pants and shirts pieced and sewn together.

Tom loses his pant leg (above) in support of his favorite Salvage Sister.

A lovingly worn oxford-cloth shirt covers the back side of the Young family's quilt (right), with the collar, pocket, placket, and cuff left intact.

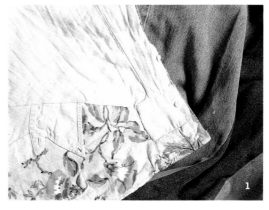

HOW TO MAKE A QUILT
FROM YOUR OLD CLOTHES

materials

SCISSORS

SEVERAL PAIRS OF DISCARDED JEANS

MEASURING TAPE

SEWING MACHINE

IRON

OLD SHIRT OR CONTRASTING FABRIC
FOR THE BACK SIDE

PRINTED FABRIC LARGE ENOUGH TO MAKE
A 4- TO 5-INCH BORDER ON BACK

COTTON OR POLYESTER QUILT BATTING

PINS

NEEDLE AND WHITE QUILTING THREAD

1. Cut several pairs of well-worn jeans, corduroys, khakis, or other sturdy pants that your family wears into pieces of varying sizes (photograph 2). This quilt features mostly rectangles measuring anything from 2 by 24 inches to 4 by 24 inches. Note that many of the pieces are not perfect rectangles. Arrange the pieces on the floor in a pleasing "undesigned" pattern, alternating shades and degrees of wear throughout. You may want to piece together a few shapes at a time rather than arrange all of your fabric at the beginning. This will allow for a more serendipitous design.

2. Depending on the size of the quilt you want to make (this one is approximately 4 feet by 6 feet), machine stitch the pieces together with the right sides facing each other and $\frac{1}{4}$-inch seams to prevent bulk. Open out the pieces and press the seams flat to one side. When all the pieces have been joined, trim

around the edges to make them somewhat even (or slightly uneven, like Mary Ann's, which adds to the charm).

3. To make the back side, choose a somewhat contrasting fabric to give your quilt an element of surprise (photograph 1). Mary Ann used a long-sleeved button-down shirt left whole and kept the buttons, shirt pocket, and placket on it. She sewed strips of floral fabric from an old pair of pants around the shirt to make the back side $1\frac{1}{4}$ inches larger than the front on each side.

4. Lay the front of the quilt on a work surface (or the floor) wrong side up. Place a piece of quilt batting on top of it, then lay the back piece over it right side up (photograph 3).

5. Turn the quilt over so that the top is right side up. Fold the excess fabric from the bottom piece over the top piece, turn under $\frac{1}{4}$ inch and pin to secure (photograph 4). Hand or machine stitch around the edge of the quilt to create a border. Hand stitch the layers together using white quilting thread and a running stitch in geometric patterns. The more patterns, the better!

This graphic patchwork quilt is the kids' favorite blanket—not least because it's made from their parents' well-worn jeans and corduroys. But the softness of their dad's old cotton button-down, sewn into the backside, is what really makes them smile.

shredded-silk curtains

For hippies at heart:
Where have all the beaded curtains gone?

Silk strips are the Salvage Sisters' answer to the beaded curtain. The minute Kathleen and her husband, Stephen, walked into the empty parlor-floor apartment in Brooklyn, they were sold. The hardwood floors had aged to an ugly gold, the period molding was gone, the marble fireplace was covered in fifteen coats of paint, and the kitchen was a mass-produced logistical mess. Within seconds, they redid the rooms in their heads, envisioning how they could make the most of the fourteen-foot ceilings and those cut-rate kitchen cupboards. It's all cosmetic, they repeated to themselves. Almost a year later, their ideas had become a reality—with the exception of that dingy kitchen, a work in progress. So rather than subject themselves—and their frequent guests—to a less-than-appetizing view of the kitchen, Kathleen shredded lengths of silk to make a sweeping curtain that they can walk through and hide eyesores behind.

HOW TO MAKE A SHREDDED-SILK CURTAIN

For impact and depth, choose three hues in the same color family. We chose salmon, peach, and terra-cotta, all variations of the color orange. Apple green, sage, and avocado or any other combination of monochromatic colors will achieve the same effect. Using a lightweight fabric such as silk will allow the curtain to flow in the lightest breeze—and it's easier to snip and tear.

materials

SILK FABRIC IN THREE DIFFERENT COLORS

SCISSORS

BAMBOO ROD OR DOWEL

CUP HOOKS LARGE ENOUGH TO HOLD THE ROD

1. Measure the width and length of the doorway or opening you want to cover.

2. Buy three different-color fabrics in yard lengths equal to the height of your doorway or opening plus about 4 inches to allow for tying the strips to the rod and that ever-important flourish on the floor. For example, we bought 3¼ yards of each fabric to cover a 9-foot-high opening.

3. Working along the short end of the fabric, snip 1 inch into it at 1½-inch intervals.

4. Put your scissors away and start ripping! Tear strips along the entire length of the fabric, laying each one over the back of a chair as you go—the strips get tangled easily, so handle them gingerly.

5. To attach the strips to a rod, hang the rod in a convenient spot at shoulder height. Tie the strips onto the rod with a simple knot, randomly choosing the colors as you go.

6. To hang the curtain, screw 2 cup hooks about 3 inches in from either side of the doorway or opening, making sure to center them. Hang the curtain by setting the rod into the hooks, then step right through it.

A dramatic floor-length curtain covers up a kitchen renovation in progress. On the chairs, a vintage dress delivers more style on the seats than it ever did on its owner (page 88).

swingin' seat covers

Stretch fabric from a groovy vintage dress over simple square chairs.

In Brooklyn, many streets are lined with brownstones boasting the imposing stoops that give their neighborhoods distinctive architectural significance. Sounds pretty highbrow, doesn't it? Maybe so, but the people who live in these beautiful buildings aren't shy about making a buck or two while sitting on their exquisite steps. On most Saturdays, as soon as the snow melts, you will find Brooklynites setting up shop on their stairs—the urban version of a yard sale. In fact, on one Sunday every fall, the borough celebrates the revival of famed Atlantic Avenue, now lined with boutiques and antiques shops, with the Atlantic Antic, a mile-long street fair. Savvy Brooklynites on either side of the avenue take advantage of the crowds by putting everything but the kitchen sink up for sale. That's where we picked up these ugly chairs with the nice lines. With a couple of coats of paint and some new seat covers cut from one of Kathleen's vintage linen dresses (it made her stick out in all the wrong places), we gave them such an invigorating makeover that their former owner might not recognize them. (Note: A Salvage Sister never upholsters anything more complicated than these chairs.)

HOW TO COVER THE SEAT OF A CHAIR

materials

OLD DRESS

CHAIRS

SCREWDRIVER

PINS

STAPLE GUN

1. If you're using an old dress, cut it flat on the floor in whatever way yields the largest piece as possible. We cut this dress on the zipper seam. You may need to cut off the upper part of a shaped bodice just under the armholes.

2. Unscrew the seats from the chairs using a screwdriver (or in our case, a butter knife). Remove the old covering and use it as your template for the new one. Pin the old seat cover to the new fabric and cut out a seat cover for each chair.

3. Lay the new seat cover on a work surface wrong side up. Set the seat on it, top side down. Working one side at a time, pull the fabric onto the bottom of the seat and, using a staple gun, fasten it to the seat. Repeat on the opposite side, followed by the two remaining sides. Pay extra attention to the corners—smooth them before stapling.

4. Screw the chair seats back in place.

decorating don'ts

Avoid the expected, Salvage Sister.

At first glance, you may find this room appealing, but it could be *so* much more so. Let's start with the curtains. It's not the pattern, it's the placement of them that gets us going. Why cover up handsome old window casings—and weigh down the whole room—with yards and yards of fabric that doesn't really give you much privacy or panache? These windows would be better dressed in no-nonsense flat shades to let a little light shine in when you want it to and shield you from the world when you don't. Moving on to the chairs: Sometimes symmetry is not the answer. Two of the same chairs under identical windows aren't very expressive, and unless you use them as time-out chairs, these probably wouldn't get sat on much. And that mirror? What's it doing there? How about a tiny painting instead?

What to lose first? It's a toss-up, but those curtains have got to go . . . to the ball. Take a peek at the following pages and then read on.

Although we cut out our duds freehand, simple patterns—look through the *Vogue* pattern book first—are available at your local fabric store. Or, fashion them from favorite clothing you already own (the necktie was cut using an existing one).

What to do with a boring by-the-book room arrangement? Take a few chances.

Maria von Trapp has nothing
on the Salvage Sisters. From
left: Mary Jane wears a hip
halter dress and head scarf,
Jackie (the dog) shows off a
new collar, Tom beams in
a big bow tie, Tom Tom sports
a pair of surf shorts, Mary Ann
glows in a floor-length gown,
Kathleen makes herself at
home in a maxi skirt, Stephen
stands tall in a frayed tie, and
Finn dons a designer diaper.

dapper dog sweater

Jackie, we hardly know ye in that chic sweater.

Mary Ann's Jack Russell, Jackie, is top dog. His every need is attended to, especially his seasonal wardrobe. When winter rolls around, he's never left out in the cold. On the contrary, he's coddled in cashmere. Now, we're not suggesting you shell out for a soft sheath at one of those fancy doggie boutiques; rather, go shopping in the back of your closet. That's where we shove all of the clothes we wish worked. Take, for instance, the orange cashmere turtleneck sweater Kathleen bought at an end-of-season sale. She never, ever wore it. It was too boxy, and, the color made her skin look green. Not convinced it would never morph into that fitted silhouette she was looking for, she hung on to it—until Jackie entered the picture, that is. With a single swipe of the scissors, she had the beginnings of his winter wear.

A sweater sleeve makes a cozy
cover-up for Jack (opposite).
A personalized one ensures his
pals won't forget his name (left).

HOW TO MAKE A DOG SWEATER FROM THE SLEEVE OF YOUR SWEATER

Choose a sweater with sleeves that suit the size of your dog. (A good-size Lab might wear a men's large, say, and a cocker spaniel a ladies' medium.)

materials

SCISSORS

SWEATER

EMBROIDERY NEEDLE BIG ENOUGH TO ACCOMMODATE YARN

YARN

TAILOR'S CHALK

1. Using a sharp pair of scissors, cut off one sleeve from the sweater along the ridge that is formed where it meets the bodice.

2. Hold the sleeve up to your dog, with the wrist opening near his or her neck and the armpit opening stretching to just in front of the hind legs. Eyeball where the front legs need to slide through, keeping in mind that to make a turtleneck, you'll need a bit of extra length on the wrist end to fold back. Cut holes in the sweater for your dog's front legs.

3. Try the sweater on your dog and trim the length in the back to custom fit your pooch. (If you want to personalize your dog's sweater, read on.)

HOW TO STITCH YOUR DOG'S NAME ONTO A SWEATER

1. Match your needle size to the weight of your yarn (the wool should slip easily through the eye of the needle).

2. Using tailor's chalk, write your pet's name where you want it to be placed on the sweater.

3. Thread the yarn through the needle and tie a knot in one end. Bring the needle up from the wrong side of the sweater to the right side at the beginning of the first letter (photograph 1).

4. Hold down the yarn on the sweater's surface with the end of your thumb about 1/4 inch away from where the yarn came up, following the chalk line. Insert the needle back in the hole the yarn came up through, forming a loop. Pull the yarn fairly taut, still holding the loop down with your thumb. Bring the needle back up at the point where your thumb is, catching the loop (photograph 2).

5. Continue stitching this way to form a chain that follows the chalk line you've drawn. Finish your chain stitch with a simple knot.

couture coat

Prêt-à-porter, almost; from Gap to gorgeous.

For our money, there's always a way to make an off-the-rack raincoat look like a one-of-a-kind creation. What inspired us to turn this khaki version into a field of flowers? Must have been those clear plastic rain hats with the floating flowers in them that we wore as little girls. These plastic flowers (hey, they're waterproof) are available at craft stores. Add a simple detail to the cuff and you'll be looking swell, rain or shine.

1. With a needle and heavy-duty thread, hand sew each flower to the inside lining of the coat in an allover pattern.

2. Pull a few petals from a single flower where a button would typically go, and hand sew them together in a floral pattern on each cuff.

It's what's on the inside that makes this simple-looking coat so cool (above). The only hint of its floral lining lies on each cuff, where a few petals form a tiny flower (right).

the ten-minute chandelier

A torn silk shade is a terrible thing to toss out.

A trash-bound lamp shade with good lines has a lot of life left in it, especially if it's double lined. Within minutes, we transformed this shade into a clever and colorful chandelier by pinning varying widths of patterned and plain scraps of fabric to the inside lining with straight pins. Each piece was gently torn into strips to give the chandelier that slightly frayed look we love. We even got hung up on the cord it's hanging from. A length of fabric in a complementary color covers up the cord to give the shade a cohesive look.

Save those scraps! A colorful arrangement of fabric pieces is the perfect cover-up for a torn lampshade.

poignant pillow

An old circle skirt makes a great big bolster for your bed.

It used to be Mary Ann's favorite summer dud, not only because it's made of cool cotton, but for a more sentimental reason. She didn't know all those years ago when she bought the skirt that the text that ran along the hemline would come to sum up her married life: *A curious sailor boy appeared and took my hand, and led me only goodness knows where.* The day after they said "I do," Mary Ann and Tom set sail for the Bahamas from Lake Champlain in Vermont.

Reluctant to toss out the full-skirted mini when fashions changed, Mary Ann cut off the waistband to release the gathers into a six-foot-long piece of fabric that found a new life as a pillow that reaches across a queen-size bed.

Mary Ann says Sometimes you have to look underneath the surface for the beautiful details. Attach the skirt of a vintage ball gown around the rim of a slipcovered chair—like a petticoat—for a swank but understated detail.

Kathleen says Cut along one seam of a full skirt and wrap it around the base of your Christmas tree for an off-the-hanger tree skirt—a classic Salvage Sister move.

Cut loose from its waistband, a gathered summer skirt spans the width of a bed, making it the perfect piece of clothing to turn into a bolster pillow.

HOW TO TURN A GATHERED SKIRT INTO A BOLSTER

Though Mary Ann's skirt is likely one of a kind, any gathered skirt can be turned into a bolster for a bed, small sofa, or bench. A skirt with a border would work beautifully, but base your choice on a fabric you love or one that has sentimental value.

materials

SCISSORS

GATHERED SKIRT WITH OR WITHOUT A PRINTED BORDER

SEWING MACHINE

NEEDLE AND THREAD

POLYESTER OR DOWN FILLING

1. Use scissors to cut away the waistband from the skirt. Cut the skirt into two identical-size pieces for the shape you want.

2. With right sides together, stitch a ¾-inch seam around the rim of the rectangle, leaving a 3- to 4-inch opening on one end.

3. Turn the pillow right side out, making sure the corners have been completely turned out (it helps to trim excess fabric from the corner seams before turning). Fill the pillow with polyester or down filling (we cut open a down-filled pillow that had seen better days and reused the feathers).

4. Whipstitch the opening shut and smooth the pillow to spread the filling or feathers evenly.

a smart bow tie

So *that's* how you get to Carnegie Hall.

When you live on the coast of Maine, as Mary Ann does, you don't exactly have many formalwear sources at your fingertips. But when her son, Tom Tom, announced—just a few hours before he was due onstage for the Christmas concert— that he was supposed to wear a red tie, his mother's panic was only momentary. (Salvage Sisters don't sweat the sartorial stuff, as you can see on pages 90–91.)

Mary Ann headed for the attic, dug out a pair of old Scotch plaid pegged pants, circa 1980, and whipped out her scissors. She cut a wide swath from the left leg and fashioned a bow tie that none of Tom Tom's fellow cellists could boast. Using a trusty safety pin—one of our mother's favorite fastening methods (the other is masking tape)—Mary Ann secured it to his shirt, and in seconds the musician was dressed for his debut performance. If Tom Tom had let her, Mary Ann would have left the edges frayed, but twelve-year-olds have personal taste, you know. Use this last-minute method on grown-ups, too, as we did for big Tom's tie on pages 90–91. And you wonder why we save outdated duds?

Tom Tom is glad to be in plaid; his orchestra mates—including his sister, Mary Jane—will all be wearing solid red.

HOW TO MAKE A TWO-MINUTE BOW TIE

materials

RULER

SCISSORS

PLAID PANTS, PAJAMAS, OR ANY OTHER PIECE OF CLOTHING IN A SEASONAL WEIGHT (MADRAS IN SUMMER, FLANNEL IN WINTER)

SAFETY PIN

1. Measure and cut a 5-inch by 18-inch rectangle from an old pair of pants or other cast-off piece of clothing. Choose a fabric that is easy to manipulate—linen, cotton, or flannel, for example.

2. Fold the fabric in half lengthwise, wrong sides facing each other. Fold lengthwise again, not quite in half, so that the frayed edges fall below the first fold. The piece should measure just wider than 1 inch.

3. To make the bow, use the "rabbit ears" method you used when you first learned how to tie your shoes. Make two loops and tie them in a knot. Loosen the loops and shape the tie to suit you. Fasten a safety pin onto the back of the knot and pin the tie to a shirt collar at the neck. Grab your cello and head to the show.

She's never owned a box of holiday decorations. It's just not Mary Ann's style. Who wants the same old tree year in and year out? So when Christmas rolls around at the Youngs' house, you never know what's going to be decking the halls. One year, just the top of the tree was decorated because her children, then five and six, insisted on tossing the ornaments onto the two-story blue spruce from the library balcony above. *I'm going to leave it just like that,* Mary Ann decided. Another year, she let them choose the lights, which they excitedly determined would be blue— not necessarily their mother's ideal choice (even a Salvage Sister has her limits).

Whether fabric and feathers, tulle and tinsel, or pom-poms and paper, many of our last-minute holiday decorations are left to serendipity, and that's where newsprint comes in. *Now,* you may be asking yourself, *how could one of the most familiar—and ordinary— materials on earth make the grade on a holiday tree?* We think the more modest the supplies, the more challenging— and ultimately captivating—the results. So why not shred newspaper into strips and swathe your tree in it? It's pure Salvage Sister: uncontrived whimsy.

Be it ever so humble, there's no better destination for a Salvage Sister than the newspaper pile. Or the forest floor. Or the beach at low tide. Here is our Cartier. Our Bergdorf. Our Barneys. Give us a choice between shopping on Madison Avenue or hunting and gathering on a mile-long beach and, well, a flip through the pages in this chapter will tell you where our adrenaline is certain to flow. What is it about such often-overlooked things as rocks, pinecones, and driftwood that intrigues us in ways a shiny diamond or killer handbag never could? If you've ever suffered from buyer's remorse, you know what we're getting at.

Though we rarely regret a splurge in the shoe department, the truth is that the thrill of owning a pair of pretty heels fades faster than you can say, "I'll take them." Not so with the beautiful, useful objects we make out of lowly—but ultimately lovely—materials such as butcher paper, garden burlap, and mussel shells.

Whether out of necessity or passion or a little bit of both, trimming a Christmas tree with skinny shreds of newspaper, scavenging a beautifully weather-beaten board from a construction site and hanging it over a window for a valance, or clothing a barren dress form in a fanciful skirt made from mussel shells offers more—and more lasting—emotional and visual impact than purchasing anything new.

Perhaps more than in other chapters, the projects in this section rely on ingenuity rather than fancy do-it-yourself skills. A glue gun and a few grade-school craft techniques are the most we ask of you—with one or two exceptions. In fact, reimagining the backdrop for a pile of sticks, a bed of rocks, or the Sunday comics and elevating these items to works of art asks far more of your creative reserves than being a skilled whipstitcher or having a steady hand with a drill. When you can envision a stack of newspapers as clever, chic, and recyclable decorations, you're a true Salvage Sister.

good news holiday garland

For holiday decorations, read, rip, and rejoice.

Why limit yourself to *wrapping gifts* with newspaper when you can cover the whole room in it? When it's time to deck the halls for the holidays, we don't have to hunt down our decorations in the back of a closet or the outer reaches of the attic. We simply raid the newspaper-recycling bin, and in an afternoon, the tree is ready and the wreath is on the wall. With all of the materials we need at our fingertips, we never have to face the madding crowds, not to mention the maddening prices of predictable garlands and other ornamentation. Nothing stops us in our tracks like a look that's clever, simple to make, and chic—like a tree swathed in skinny strips of newsprint or a wreath made entirely of the stuff—bow and all. The best part? There's no deadly session of dismantling the decorations and packing them up once the holidays are over. Kathleen takes the whole tree—garland and all—to the community mulch in her neighborhood. Mary Ann, on the other hand, always uses a live tree that the family plants when the holidays are over (consult your local nursery for instructions on doing this yourself). She simply returns the garland to the recycling pile.

Santa can't believe his eyes; this simply decorated tree is big news.

HOW TO MAKE A NEWSPAPER GARLAND FOR THE TREE

The secret to making the strips look so casually arranged is to pay extra attention to how you do it. As with most decor that looks a bit tossed off, this undone effect requires a sharp eye. The placement is actually very calculated, with each cluster of strips arranged as if it were a section of wide ribbon. Make your shreds as wide or narrow as the style of your tree dictates: We used a fir tree with tight branches, so we gave the garland a loose look to complement them. For a 6-foot tree, you'll need about 25 to 30 spread-open sheets of newspaper.

materials

SCISSORS

SEVERAL NEWSPAPER SPREADS

RULER

1. Using sharp scissors, cut across the width of a stack of 4 newspaper spreads into ½-inch-wide strips (any fatter and you'll strip the tree of its grace and movement). Repeat until you have enough clusters of strips to cover your tree.

2. Gather 4 strips at a time and loosely weave them through the tree's branches (rather than pulling them taut). Continue working around the tree as you would with a traditional garland, leaving 3 to 4 inches between a strand of garland and the ones above and below it. Sit back and admire your handiwork.

With streamers down to *there*, a playful wreath made from humble newsprint tells a Salvage Sister story.

recycled wreath

A "green" wreath that's the easiest one on earth to make.

Any circular design makes a wreath, but the beauty of this one is not only that newspaper is used to make it, but the five-foot-long bow is fashioned from the same stuff. We made the newspaper florets the same way we learned how to make tissue-paper flowers at camp.

HOW TO MAKE A NEWSPAPER WREATH

materials
SCISSORS
RULER
SEVERAL NEWSPAPER SPREADS
PINKING SHEARS
FINE-GAUGE FLORAL WIRE
HOT-GLUE GUN
24-INCH PLASTIC-FOAM WREATH FORM

1. For a 24-inch wreath, you'll need 40 flowers. To make a flower, cut 4-inch by 4-inch squares from a stack of 3 spreads of newspaper. With 3 squares neatly aligned, fold the stack like an accordion, making $1/2$-inch folds as you go (photograph 1).

2. Trim the edges with pinking shears. Twist a length of fine-gauge floral wire around the middle of the accordion, leaving just enough wire to allow you to hold the flower comfortably in your hand (photograph 2).

3. Gently spread the accordion folds and lift the petals one by one toward the center of the flower. Clip the wire to $1/4$ inch (photograph 3).

4. Using a hot-glue gun, apply a bit of glue to the back side of the flower and, working from the inner ring out (you will have 3 rings), attach the flowers until the entire surface of the wreath form is covered.

5. To make the bow, cut five $1^1/2$-inch-wide by 12-inch-long strips from the paper. Form a loop with each strip, then gather up all 5 loops like a bouquet of flowers. Secure them together with a length of floral wire.

6. To make the streamers, pull one sheet from the newspaper and position the short side so that it is facing you. Fold it as you would an accordion, making $3/4$-inch folds as you go. Cut the piece crosswise into four $1^1/2$-inch-wide pieces. Unfold each piece. Connect one strip to another if you want longer streams. Attach the streamers to the back of the bow using a hot-glue gun. Apply an ample amount of hot glue to the back of the bow and attach it to the bottom center of the wreath.

witty wall decoration

A funny thing happened to Tom Tom's comics.

For those of you who always have fresh flowers on hand or a bountiful supply of evergreens, you might want to skip this one. For the rest of you, there's no need to stoop to plastic arrangements (not to mention subjecting your neighbors and friends to them) or live with none at all. Just wait until everyone in the family has read his or her favorite Sunday comic strip, get out your scissors and go to town! Not only is the colorful newsprint eye-catching, but when it's turned into a cool piece of art, it'll get the conversation going.

No wind is necessary to enjoy the whimsy of these kaleidoscopically colored pinwheels arranged around a wreath form (opposite).

Mary Jane plays the cutup, sneaking squares of Tom Tom's comics from right out under his nose (below).

HOW TO MAKE A COMIC STRIP PINWHEEL WREATH

materials

SCISSORS

RULER

SEVERAL NEWSPAPER SPREADS OF COMICS

STRAIGHT PINS

10-INCH PLASTIC-FOAM WREATH FORM

1. Cut ten 4-inch squares from the comic strip spreads.

2. Working with one square at a time, fold it in half diagonally and in half again, then unfold.

3. Cut along each crease two-thirds of the way toward the square's center, dividing each corner into two points.

4. Bring every other point to the center so that they overlap. Holding the points in place, poke a straight pin through the center, being sure to catch all the points.

5. Attach the pinwheel to the wreath form using the same pin. Repeat these instructions with the remaining squares until the entire surface of the form is covered.

old mirror makeover
Take a page from the Arts section.

When Mary Ann and Tom bought the place they affectionately call The House That Nobody Wanted, there wasn't a stick of furniture left behind worth salvaging, nor was there any molding worth saving. The only orphaned object with any potential was a tiny Chippendale-style mirror with old glass that was left hanging over the bathroom sink. The small scale was charming, but the style was too stuffy for us (see it in its original form on page 89). When in doubt, we always turn to our signature decorating material, newspaper. We'd upholster our chairs in it if we could.

To breathe new life into the fussy mirror frame, we gave it a black-and-white newspaper veneer, then added a color photo at the crown and in each corner. Curiously, just days after we mounted the newspaper print of Picasso's *Boy with a Pipe* onto the frame, the original painting fetched the most money in history at Sotheby's auction house. With a one-dollar copy of *The New York Times* and a bit of glue, we get to enjoy Picasso's genius, too, without spending a fortune.

The color pages of the newspaper begot the crinkled balls in each urn, while a combination of color and black-and-white newsprint gave a fussy mirror a finer look.

HOW TO APPLY NEWSPAPER TO A FRAME

Covering a simple square frame is easier than covering one with a decorative scroll like ours, but the steps are the same.

materials

MIRROR
CARDBOARD STOCK
PENCIL
SCISSORS
NEWSPAPER
CRAFT GLUE
UTILITY KNIFE

1. Lay the mirror on cardboard stock, trace around the decorative crown, and cut out the shape. This will be your pattern.

2. Place the pattern on a piece of newspaper, trace around the pattern, and cut the shape out of the newspaper.

3. Brush a thin layer of glue onto the crown and smooth the newspaper over it.

4. To cover the simple square rim, cut strips from the newspaper that are slightly wider than the frame. Working with one strip at a time, apply a thin layer of glue to one side of the frame, center the strip on it, and smooth it out.

5. Using a utility knife, trim away the excess newspaper.

6. In each corner, we placed iconic images of home—a bouquet and an urn, for example. To add color, we centered Picasso's masterpiece on the crown and glued it there. You can cut out your favorite featured masterpiece or news event, too.

Who needs houndstooth
when mussel shells glued
this way and that give a
dress form great texture?

mussel shell mini

Can't shell out the dough for pricey sculpture?

Skip the galleries and go shelling instead. Never know what to do with those beach treasures once you're home from vacation? We use ours to make shell art, Salvage Sister style. Our aging dress form needed a fashion makeover, so we designed a skirt of weathered and dried mussel, oyster, and scallop shells to give it a fresh look. Now the once-attic-bound piece is a humble but intriguing presence in Mary Ann's dressing area. You don't have to have a dress form to enjoy the beauty of shells, though. Cover a mirror or picture frame, the top of a table, or the back of a chair with them. Or glue them in an appealing pattern right on the wall!

HOW TO COVER A DRESS FORM
IN SHELLS

materials
DRESS FORM
HOT-GLUE GUN
SHELLS

1. Remove the wire cage of the dress form, if desired.

2. Clean the surface of the dress form with a damp cloth.

3. Using a hot-glue gun, apply glue to shells one at a time and attach each in a single row around the hemline of the dress form.

4. Continue applying shells in rows, overlapping with the previous row, until the entire bodice is covered.

5. Add decorative accents such as shell jewelry, around the chest, neck, and waist, if desired.

Not ones to waste a single shell, we arranged a combination of oyster and mussel shells around the form's waist to make a beautiful belt. Because we couldn't help ourselves, we embellished it with a pair of mother-of-pearl earrings.

love notes

A simple rock sends a poignant message if you put it in the right place.

Perhaps it's the flat surface of the rocks we pick up, or maybe just a fond memory of a summer-camp craft, but whatever the reason, we love the innocent charm of painted rocks. Sure, you can use them as paperweights or doorstops, but wouldn't it be wonderful to place one in an unexpected—even banal—spot? We've put them on the shower floor, around the tub drain, in the laundry-soap bin, in an underwear drawer, and even in a lunch box.

Red paint on a rock says it all in Kathleen's husband's top drawer.

A few of their favorite things greet the Young family whenever they do the dishes. A dog, house, crab, and the Salvage Sisters—all rendered in acrylic paint—won't wear off when the water hits them.

A plain old four-poster can go from fuddy-duddy to fabulous with the simple addition of a few pinecone bouquets.

fancy finials

Wake up a four-poster bed with pinecones from the forest floor.

You don't have to go camping under the stars to bring a little of the great outdoors into your life. But if nature's not your thing, almost anything goes on these four posts, except for bowling balls, maybe.

Mary Ann says Plug in your glue gun and line up those pinecones along the top of the headboard. If you really want to raise it to the roof, extend the headboard by sliding a piece of plywood behind your bed (secure with picture hooks) and gluing pinecones all over it.

Kathleen says What? You're a minimalist? Just place a single chubby pinecone on each post for a streamlined touch.

HOW TO MAKE FLEUR-DE-LIS PINECONE FINIALS

materials

PAINT TO MATCH THE COLOR OF YOUR BEDPOSTS

4 SHALLOW BOTTLE CAPS

FINE-GAUGE FLORAL WIRE

12 TALL PINECONES

HOT-GLUE GUN

REMOVABLE DOUBLE-FACED TAPE

1. Paint each bottle cap in a color close to that of the wood of your bedposts.

2. Wire together 3 pinecones at their bases. Continuing to work in groups of 3, repeat with the remaining pinecones.

3. Fill a bottle cap with hot glue and set a trio of pinecones in it. Hold the pinecones firmly until the glue dries. Repeat with the 3 remaining finials.

4. Mount a finial on each post, securing it with double-faced tape (which allows you to remove the finial without pulling the finish off the bed).

"In all things of nature there is something of THE MARVELOUS."

—Aristotle

and so to bed

Go to sleep with this lofty thought.

Put a stack of pallets—as high as you like—underneath a mattress, and you'll sleep like a prince or princess. Pallets are as ubiquitous as shopping carts—yet you never knew you had any use for them. Those wooden pallets that transfer groceries from the delivery truck to the supermarket make great bed frames; they raise the mattress off the floor and eliminate the need for a box spring. We like them placed directly on the floor and stacked about three feet high, with a mattress on top.

"Give them
what THEY NEVER KNEW
they wanted."

—Diana Vreeland

However high you pile them, pallets stack up to Salvage Sister style: They're free, fun, and fabulous looking.

There's no guessing what language is spoken in this house. Driftwood says it all.

Salvage Sister sign language

All you need is L-O-V-E
and a few sticks to get you started.

It all started with an L-shaped piece of driftwood. What other letters might be floating out there, just waiting to wash ashore and spell something? That single letter was all it took for us to set out in search of yet more driftwood. Finding a V wasn't so hard, but an E? Mary Ann just happened to find a worn stick that, when held just so, perfectly resembled that vowel. As for the O, well, we cheated a bit by winding grapevines clipped from a tangle in the backyard. Placed in a bare spot on Mary Ann's side porch, the sweet sentiment makes passersby stop and smile. And depending on the season, the O gets a different decoration, from a tiny evergreen bough during winter to a few sprigs of bittersweet when the leaves begin to change.

flotsam for your walls

Washed-up pieces of wood
make a whale of a family on a wall.

(pages 122-123)

In the same spirit that we, as children, saw the outlines of horses, dogs, and Aunt Alice in the clouds in the sky, we often pick up pieces of driftwood that mimic the shapes of states, animals, and, of course, letters. On one trip, we found several smooth gray pieces that were worn into the shape of whales. We brought the priceless pieces of folk art home and hung them in a pod on the living-room wall.

Finn goes on his first whale watch and spots three—the father, mother, and their baby.

palatial mirror

Found art is the most fabulous kind of all.

An inveterate collector of the soft gray wood whose rough texture has been smoothed by saltwater, Mary Ann has been known to haul twenty-five-pound pieces onto the family sailboat. Not that this should surprise fellow Salvage Sisters. On day sails, overnight trips, and even multiweek vacations, she's always picked up driftwood whenever she comes upon it. It's only this brand of passion for things most people pass over that will get you a museum-quality mirror framed in beautifully weathered wood. A summer's worth of picking up sticks and pieces is represented around the mirror's rim, a charming reminder of the places visited only by boat. Though perfect resting on the mantel in a Maine house, the over-the-top presence of the piece could make it the focal point in a city apartment, too. Kathleen's been trying to barter her shredded-silk curtain (page 86) for this for months, but we've decided to share custody, as any Salvage Sister would.

HOW TO MAKE A DRIFTWOOD MIRROR

We intentionally glued the pieces of driftwood to the mirror to make them look as though they washed up on it. We always want the pieces to look natural and wouldn't dream of trimming them to fit.

materials

SIMPLE FRAMED MIRROR

LOTS OF DRIFTWOOD

HOT-GLUE GUN

1. If you are covering a frame as large as this one, place the mirror where you plan to have it permanently, then glue the sticks on it one piece at a time. Allow some branches to spill onto the glass and others to stretch beyond the confines of the frame.

2. To make the "coat of arms" at the top, we positioned the last two sticks in a wide X and glued them on top of the other driftwood pieces.

Mary Ann says Make a truly evergreen holiday tree—one that will last forever—by stacking graduated lengths of driftwood in a triangular shape and nailing them together.

Kathleen says Gather up an armload of driftwood of various lengths and arrange them—askew, of course—in a big bucket as you would fresh flowers for a soothing bouquet.

HOW TO MAKE PAPER FLOWERS EVERLASTING

Instead of fresh flowers, pick up some colorful paper and sticks. Cut decorative wrapping paper into imperfect circles, stack three or four pieces, and puncture them through the center of the circle with floral wire. Hot glue them to varying lengths of sticks for a perennial bouquet.

A one-of-a-kind mirror is all a mantel needs to make it magical. Here, driftwood in all shapes and lengths covers the frame while two pieces at the top form a stately crest.

When fresh flowers can't be
found, pick up some paper
and sticks. Make simple buds
and glue them to wooden
"stems."

"*For all the things we*
TWIST, TEAR, AND TOSS OUT;
*for all the things we
think little or nothing of;
for all the things
that pass through our hands,
mouths, and fingers—
there is . . . a possibility of
aesthetic* **SALVAGE.**"

—Tara Donovan, installation artist

signature swing

It doesn't matter how you get that huge piece of driftwood home, just get it.

And then turn it into a two-seater seaside swing. Despite its heft, we couldn't resist the perfectly weathered beam that had washed ashore on an uninhabited island in Penobscot Bay. It took only seconds to size it up as the perfect bench swing for Mary Ann's side porch. We dragged it to the dinghy, rowed it out to the boat, and sailed it home. Now it's become the favorite place for Tom Tom and Mary Jane to wait for friends to come and play.

HOW TO TURN A DRIFTWOOD BEAM INTO A SWING

materials

1-INCH DRILL BIT AND A SECOND DRILL BIT SLIGHTLY SMALLER THAN THE SHAFT OF THE SCREW EYE

ELECTRIC DRILL/DRIVER

4-FOOT BY 8-INCH BY 4-INCH PIECE OF DRIFTWOOD (FOR A DOUBLE SWING)

MEASURING TAPE

24 FEET OF ⅝-INCH-THICK NYLON ROPE

SCISSORS

8-INCH SCREW EYES

1. Using a 1-inch drill bit, drill a hole in either end of a length of driftwood, about 4 inches from each end and centered.

2. Cut the rope into two 12-foot-long pieces. Thread one rope through each hole in the driftwood and knot the rope on the underside using a bowline knot (right) or other load-bearing knot.

3. Using a drill bit that is slightly smaller than the shaft of the screw eye, drill holes into a beam (or wherever you will hang the swing from) approximately 40 inches apart and centered. Begin screwing screw holes using your hands. When it becomes difficult to continue turning, slide a screwdriver through the screw eyes and use it as a torque to twist the screw eye securely into the beam.

4. Thread the loose end of each rope through an eye, adjust for desired height, and fasten the rope to itself using another bowline knot.

HOW TO TIE A BOWLINE KNOT

The bowline knot is ideal for a swing because it doesn't tighten or loosen under strain. It's easy to undo, too, because it doesn't get entangled or wound around the rope. Here's how to make one:

1. The standing end of the rope forms "the tree." Form a loop at the end of the rope (the "rabbit hole").

2. Form a second loop (the rabbit hops out of its hole . . .).

3. Put the loose end through the loop (. . . goes around the tree). Tighten and you're done (. . . and back down the hole).

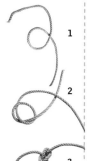

Tom Tom turns the double swing into a triple-seater, giving Jackie and his new cousin, Finn, their first swing into summer.

An invitation for all to join in the fun (opposite) is hand painted across the seat of the swing.

whimsical window cover

A naive painting on butcher paper makes a perfect summer window shade.

Rather than hang a cliché café curtain in the window, Mary Ann deftly displays Tom Tom's artwork and gets some privacy, too. What more natural a subject could there be for a seaside home in the summer? The scuba scene as imagined by her little boy brought so much joy to Mary Ann that she taped it right into the window. The paper is thick enough to shut out nosy neighbors, yet transparent enough to let the light in.

Mary Ann says Roll a length of butcher paper right off the bolt and onto your dining-room table for a priceless runner.

Kathleen says Roll letter-size pieces of butcher paper into cones and fill them with nuts, olives, popcorn, or crudités and offer one to each of your guests.

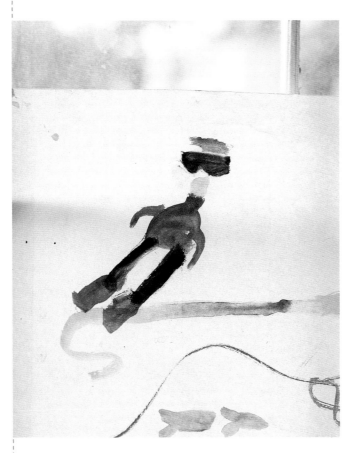

Butcher paper lets the sun shine in on a child's charming painting (opposite).

A scuba diver surveys the scene on the ocean floor in Tom Tom's painting-turned-privacy curtain.

Don't be afraid to pound a piece of wood over any window. This aged piece makes a beautiful trim.

clever cornices

Construction site cast-offs make exquisite window dressings.

Okay, so it's not every day that you're milling around a construction site. But chances are you know someone who is familiar with these $3\frac{1}{2}$-foot by 10-inch form boards, which are used to mark off the area where a foundation is to be poured. Why are we so enamored of them? The cement-encrusted planks have a patina that is positively stunning. And when they're mounted over windows, the effect is dramatic.

HOW TO MOUNT A CEMENT
FORM BOARD—OR OTHER WOODEN
VALANCE—OVER YOUR WINDOW

materials

TWO 3-INCH-LONG PIECES OF WOOD,
OR SPACERS, CUT THE SAME THICKNESS
AS THE WINDOW CASINGS

ELECTRIC DRILL/DRIVER

CEMENT FORM BOARD CUT TO
DESIRED LENGTH

FINISHING NAILS

1. Position the 2 spacers over the window casing to align with the wall studs. Drill a pilot hole (a hole slightly smaller in diameter than the nails that will attach the valance) through the spacer and into the stud.

2. Center the cement form board so that it is flush with the bottom edge of the window casing (you will cover up the casing) and fasten it to the wall with finishing nails through the spacers.

curtain call

Hang garden burlap in your windows for a superchic look on the cheap.

You see it wrapped around the roots of trees in transit, but we'd rather unfurl a roll and hang it in floor-to-ceiling windows or cut it into café curtains—anything to experience the exquisite light that filters through its rough weave.

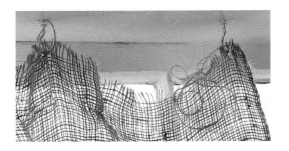

Simple cup hooks replace a curtain rod for hanging burlap curtains in tall windows.

"Fringed" curtains in
Mary Ann's dining room
are casually hung over
lengths of fine wire tacked
across the window frame.

In Kathleen's living room, lengths of burlap pinned back with exaggerated ball-fringe tiebacks hang elegantly in the windows. A monocled Mr. Peanut (Mary Ann has been known as "Peanut" all her life) gives the monochromatic palette a dash of invigorating color and keeps the spirit of her Salvage Sister nearby.

ACKNOWLEDGMENTS

Imagine having the opportunity to publicly thank all of the people who have made your life great. Here it is, my chance … There are those who I've had the great fortune to call loved ones and friends, and their indelible spirit is with me even when they're not. Mary Ann Young (Peanut to me!), my sister—in salvage and real life—is my best friend, too. I do not know anyone else who possesses such a rare combination of character, grace, wisdom, and unbridled determination. And she's hysterically funny, too. These qualities are matched only by the extraordinary brand of optimism that radiates from her husband, Tom. For them, I am very grateful. Mary Jane and Tom Tom Young, my niece and nephew, have been a source of ecstasy and solace since the day they were born. Thank you, Pea, for sharing your incredible and spirited family with me.

My deepest gratitude goes to Stephen Antonson, my husband and true love, who sees the world through kaleidoscopically colored glasses. Thank you. Finn James, our little boy, deserves a great big thank-you, too, for being born so good natured. One day we'll cut your hair. I am especially indebted to Namrata Pradhan, whose boundless joy and uncompromising care have made Finn's first two years magical.

In the more than ten years that I have lived in New York City, I have met hundreds of memorable people, but among them are those who I wish to thank for enriching my life in indescribable ways: Laurie Cearley, Christopher Hirsheimer, Joelle Hoverson, Fritz Karch, Lauren Holden-Kilbane, Linda Kocur, Heather Smith MacIsaac, Megan Newman, Page Marchese Norman, Ann Richman, Todd Rosenberg, Leslie Wellott, Maria Wisdom, and Martha Stewart.

Kathleen Hackett
Brooklyn, New York

My sister Kathleen has been my "it girl" throughout my life. She is the ultimate collaborative partner; her opinion is golden. Kathleen's over-the-top generosity of spirit, constant humor, and overflow of ideas are among her greatest qualities and the most treasured gifts she has given to me. She's also just a blast to be around. Thank you, Kathleen, for your hard work, determination, and many kindnesses. But most important, thank you for always believing in me. Now will you trade your shredded-silk curtain with me?

I have been fortunate to spend all of my life with spirited and loving family and friends. They have been especially invaluable to me throughout this fast-paced and all-consuming project. Tremendous thanks to my dear husband, Tom, who shared his can-do attitude and talent every step of the way. You are my shining light! And to my children, Mary Jane and Tom Tom (and Jackie, our Jack Russell, too), who are my greatest sources of inspiration and joy. Thank you, too, to Stephen Antonson, my brother-in-law and friend. He is a fine addition to our family, and his artistic hand will never cease to delight us. And of course, my newest nephew, Finn James, who I simply adore. Special thanks to A. Appleton for her prized critique; Amanda Anderson and Jessica Anderson for their friendship; J. Seidel for her humor, daily inquiries, and concern; and to Bethie Storey for her contagious enthusiasm. To all of the staff at the Maine Medical Center: Dr. Morris, Mary Ann Waterman, Maury Hill, and Mary Zamripa, who help me care for my son, Tom Tom, who struggles daily with juvenile type I diabetes. They have been my life support over the last five years. Thank you ever so much.

Mary Ann Young
Rockport, Maine

And of course . . .

Writing a book for the first time requires undaunted determination and vast reserves of good humor. If it were not for our mother and father, Robert and Jean Hackett, who instilled in us the value of having these qualities, the Salvage Sisters would still be dinner table conversation. Thank you, Mother and Dad, for telling us that we could do anything and for teaching us to see the beauty in everything. A standing ovation to our sisters and brothers, who, together with us, are thicker than thieves. There's not only safety, but an exponentially greater range of possibilities, in numbers!

Creating a book full of words and pictures is usually a bit like conducting an orchestra. In our case, it was more like an ensemble. Our numbers were limited (and so was our budget), and as a result, everyone went above and beyond the call of duty, for which we are so appreciative. Thank you to photographer Laura Moss, who made the trip to Maine in the off-season, and to the indefatigable Russell Kaye and Sandra Lee Phipps, who gamely and graciously took photographs, including those for the front and back jacket and cover, at the eleventh hour. Our husbands' talents and skills were and always will be invaluable to us. Thank you, Stephen and Tom. Mary Jane and Tom Tom Young did what comes naturally to them by lending a helping (and often clever) hand whenever we asked. A special thank-you to photo assistant Jamie Antonson, who is always entertaining to be around.

Our agent, Angela Miller, adopted this little project immediately and promptly turned around and sold it to the most elegant illustrated-book publisher in the country. Thank you, Angela, for getting us the gold ring. At Artisan, editor Pamela Cannon's enthusiasm for the book was infectious, a priceless advantage in any publishing house for first-timers like us. We are thrilled to have worked with you. Publisher Ann Bramson took excellent care of us; thank you for your attention and wisdom. Art director Vivian Ghazarian took on the not-so-small task of designing the words and layouts. Thank you for doing such a superb job. Deborah Weiss Geline wrapped her head around the Salvage Sister language and let our personalities shine through without letting us break too many rules. Many, many thanks to Peter Workman for seeing the possibilities in the Salvage Sisters. You can have a ride in the Austin Mini anytime.

Most decorating books feature photographs that have been propped with borrowed furnishings, rugs, pillows, and paintings. Not so with the Salvage Sisters. We own and live with everything you see on these pages, with the exception of the curtains on page 89, for which we thank Schumacher for supplying us with such wonderful fabric. Thank you to Hoboken Gardens for loaning us the tree in the photograph on page 104, where friend Jack Churchill stands in as Santa. A very special thank-you to Woody Emmanuel, who let us stack a mile-high pile of stuff on his just-restored car. We'd also like to thank Mother Nature for her generous supply of inspiration, and thank you to whomever threw out the ball gown on page 81.

The Salvage Sisters

notes

notes

notes

notes